Released

CHAINS TO CHOSEN

Released

CHAINS TO CHOSEN

BRANDY REYNOLDS

Join my mailing list for status updates, resources, and bonus material!

Visit:

ChainsToChosen.com

This book is dedicated to my husband, Michael, my constant anchor who balances me in the storms we've weathered. Thank you for keeping all my letters from prison, for they've turned into something.

CONTENTS

FOREWORD

By Josie Smith

A t the time I am writing this foreword, I have known Brandy for nearly twelve years. And in the time that I have known her, I have witnessed first-hand the relentlessness she possesses in her support of anyone who has found themselves in a place of brokenness—no matter how that brokenness may look on the surface. No matter how visible or invisible that brokenness may be to the outside world. Because she fully understands that no brokenness is beyond healing.

Brandy embodies what it truly means to be a servant leader. The abundance of grace, wisdom, and love which she personifies is a result of her journey of complete surrender of the brokenness she found within herself. Her strength as a leader comes from that very same grace, wisdom, and love, which she has shared with countless others through her guidance, leadership, and ministry. To have had the opportunity to walk alongside Brandy as she has spoken love, acceptance, and freedom over people through various ministry opportunities, to large groups from stages, and in intimate counseling settings has been one of the greatest gifts in my life.

To share the most vulnerable pieces of one's soul in a medium as tangible as a book such as this is one of the bravest things a person can do. To relive the darkest days of one's life through each round of writing, re-writing, editing, and re-editing has the power to bring even the strongest of souls to their knees. But Brandy has done so— not for her own benefit—but for yours, to give you hope. To give you an example of what is possible. To remind you that no matter how dark your journey may have gotten, it's never so dark that the light can't find its way in. Freedom is possible no matter where you may feel trapped in your life.

Brandy is one of the most authentically beautiful souls I've ever had the privilege of not only working alongside, but calling a friend. To be loved by Brandy is one of the greatest gifts of my life, and it's a gift I hope and pray you feel with your whole heart as you read the words she has shared on these pages because that is what I see this as—a love letter to you, the reader.

Allow yourself to be open to receiving the love that Brandy is here to extend to you. The journey you are about to embark on as you turn the page has the power to be life-changing—if you let it.

CHAPTER 1

The Sentence

September 24, 2007

I awoke that September morning and quietly slipped out of bed. I tried not to wake my husband, Michael, sleeping beside me. I wanted to watch the sun break through the darkness, for I desperately needed a breakthrough of my own. I wanted affirmation that I'd survive this day and return home. I wandered into my childhood refuge, the rock bed in front of my grandparent's home. As my fingertips touched the secret rock where their house key was hidden, I begged God to keep me safe. "I'll do whatever You ask of me, but I can do more for You outside of prison."

Time melted away. *What should I wear on the day of my sentencing?* A heaviness settled as I pictured myself standing before a judge who had complete control over the outcome of my life. His ruling affected not only me, but also those I loved. Soon I'd be stamped with a sentence, and the wait would be over.

Grandma, Mike, and I slumped into the car. I stared at my purse. *What do I need to give Mike in case I don't come back?* I reached to grab keys, credit cards, and a 3x5 card with our passwords. When I looked up, I met Mike's fear-filled eyes. I felt the familiar pressure in my chest. My heart pounded like a diesel engine firing up to run a long, hard day.

"You're singing to yourself," Grandma's voice cut through my fog. "You've always sung to yourself when you're troubled, ever since you were a little girl."

I entered the courthouse and walked down the narrow hallway filled with family and friends. My eyes swept over their long faces and pain-stricken eyes. It oddly felt like a funeral. I felt helpless. I was the encourager who could offer no comfort. I locked eyes with Todd's mom. My heart seared, thinking about how badly I'd hurt her. *Does she feel how I wish with every fiber of my being that I could take it back?*

She gently nodded and gave me a thumbs-up. I finally took in a breath of air. Her small sign gave me the strength to put one foot in front of another and stand next to my lawyer.

The judge called the room to order. With each word, the heaviness increased until I thought I'd sink through the floor. He started firing out incorrect details that waved like red flags. I whispered to my lawyer that he was wrong. My lawyer tried to intercede, but the judge had made up his mind long ago. *Did he read the letter I sent him? Can't anyone stop him? He's about to determine my life!*

"Brandy, I sentence you to four to eight years." His words were a death sentence, and I was plunged into a coffin.

The room spun, and my legs gave out. "Jesus" was all that escaped my lips as I sank into the abyss. *I know I did wrong, but this? It's too heavy; it's too much.* Someone's yelling broke the noise in my head. My dad was crying and yelling at the same time.

"I'm so sorry, Dad. I never wanted this to happen!"

When did the way lead here?

An officer came and cuffed me. I said my goodbyes to Mike and walked past my dad, who followed me out. Dad pleaded with the officers, as if they could lift the sentence of my doom. My body went through the motions like a marionette, as if someone else pulled the strings, and I watched it play out from the sidelines. I entered an elevator with guards on each side. I turned to face my broken dad as the doors closed. I could hardly breathe as thoughts raced through my mind. *I'm alone. Do they think I'm a monster? Why does it have to be this much? God, my God, why have You forsaken me?* The elevator descended.

We arrived at the bottom and exited into the county jail. I recognized the officer behind the desk, as he was my prom date from high school. It'd been a few years, but he didn't recognize me. He took my picture, much different from prom, and ushered me into a cold cell. There was a Bible that I tried to read, but I couldn't focus. I couldn't get the words to penetrate my mind. I sat on a hard bed, and my mind drifted.

How did I get here?

I met Mike on the second day of college. We sat next to each other alphabetically in history class. When he said he was from Illinois and loved the Bears, I started breaking down the Super Bowl shuffle. Grandma had later taped *The Wizard of Oz* over the shuffle, so I knew the shuffle by heart. We became fast friends. Mike pursued me with great intention. He came from a Christian family that seemed like a fairytale. He felt safe and secure, unlike anything I'd ever experienced.

Mike asked me to marry him in my junior year, and I panicked. I had no clue what a healthy marriage looked like. I'd eventually figure it out and certainly didn't want to go back home after college. We were married a few weeks after graduation.

I wanted to be near my younger sisters, so we moved into a nearby apartment. I had graduated from an unaccredited college, so there was only one school I could teach at. It was a K–12 church school an hour away. I wouldn't make much, not even minimum wage, but I was excited to start teaching. That fall, I taught a 3rd/4th-grade combination class. A family from church asked me to carpool with them. Their oldest was Todd, a sophomore in high school, and we'd take turns driving.

Because money was tight, I worked another job decorating cakes. In addition to working two jobs, I led the nursery, taught Sunday school and Wednesday night children's group, and sang in the church choir. This heavy load didn't leave much time for my new marriage. My only downtime was the two-hour car ride each day. Todd was easy to talk to, and our conversations made the time fly. He quickly deemed himself my sidekick. As the days went by, we got to know each other better.

Mike and I hung out with his best friend, Charles, and his wife, Jackie. They were married the year before us. Charles and I grew up in the same church. Charles's dad was like my second dad, calling me the daughter he never had, encouraging me when home life got difficult, and repairing a newer wrecked car for me. Charles never talked to me much growing up, so it was confusing when he wanted to talk to me alone about his struggling marriage.

I tried to be encouraging and supportive, but then Charles began acting differently toward me. One Saturday, I went over to help paint. Others were supposed to be coming, but it ended up being just Charles and me. He talked about his marriage, then backed me into the wall and tried to kiss me. Thankfully, his brother showed up, and I mumbled an excuse and slipped out the door.

Afterward, he texted me, left voicemails, and tried stopping over when Mike wasn't home. I was in shock and didn't know how to tell Mike what his best friend was doing, but I eventually showed

Mike the messages. Mike seemed to either ignore or blame me. I felt betrayed. It seemed like he cared more about Charles. Instead of talking to someone who could help, I tried to hide it and move on.

Despite my best efforts to keep matters locked up, Todd picked up on changes in my mood on the way to school. I eventually told Todd about Charles and how Mike responded. Todd had lots of suggestions about what he'd do if he were my husband. I drew comfort in someone knowing all parties involved and defending me.

As the months went by, I grew closer to Todd. The more I told him, the more I trusted him, and the closer I drew emotionally. Soon Todd and I began texting. I'm reminded of the Casting Crowns lyrics, "It's a slow fade when you give yourself away, thoughts invade, choices are made, a price will be paid when you give yourself away."[1] Little by little, I gave Todd the depth of my thoughts, feelings, and emotions.

One weekend, Mike allowed Charles to stay with us overnight. I was mad and left for our bedroom during dinner. Later, when Mike showered, Charles knocked on my door, needing a blanket. I went and grabbed one from my closet as he tried to push himself on me. I felt paralyzed, but I managed to shut him out. I told Mike what literally just happened when he got out, but he ignored me and went to sleep. I felt a wall rise between us.

The next day, I called Todd, crying, and told him. He came right over. After he arrived, he told me to go rest in bed, and I lifelessly obeyed. He told me everything would be okay as he got on top of me. I told him, "No," several times and tried to pull away.

He said, "If you won't let me, I'm still going to do it."

---

[1] "Slow Fade," *The Alter and the Door,* (Beach Street Records; Casting Crowns), 2007.

To my utter regret, I let him. I'd done all this. I'd allowed him into my world, told him everything, and gave him control. I'd crossed every line and sacrificed everything. Now he wanted something in return. Even though I said, "No," I hadn't shown him I meant it because of the actions I'd taken up to this point. I stood to blame. I was a teacher at his school and the adult.

Afterward, I functioned, but I felt numb and lifeless. Summer break came, and Todd and I avoided each other. I'd already signed up to teach my second year. Though I wanted to drive alone, we couldn't afford it. I was still upset at Todd but told myself nothing would happen again. There is no logical explanation, but I slowly allowed Todd back into my life.

Why did I continue working there? Why didn't I take a small financial hit and drive myself? Why didn't I talk to someone? I struggle to put myself back in my stupid twenty-two-year-old mind. I know what I told myself then: *I am strong enough. I was a virgin before marriage, never going to parties or trying drugs or alcohol. I'd never cheat on my husband. I've only been able to depend on myself, and I'll stay strong.* I recognize now that was pride. And as pride goes before destruction, so did my haughty spirit before my utter and devastating fall.

The story of Israel comes to mind. God rescued the Israelites from slavery. While in the wilderness, the Israelites craved the comfort they had back in Egypt. Moses reminded them they were slaves, and now they are free. They couldn't see clearly because Egypt was at the forefront of their heart and mind. They missed Egypt because it was their first-place idol. Idols always promise a release of some kind but never fully deliver and always demand more of you. You'll always need more of it. As Proverbs 26:11 says, "As a dog returns to its vomit, so a man returns to his foolishness."

The emotional affair slowly returned. I'd developed a warped dependency on Todd, much like a girl fiercely clenching her favorite doll. Dysfunctional for certain, but it felt like oxygen that I needed to breathe—a "fix," for sure. Physical intimacy soon followed, although not often. We were in the chapel every day at school and church on Sunday. It was a roller coaster trying to stay away from something I knew was extremely wrong, but afraid of what my life would be without it. I decided not to teach the following year, and our relationship soon ended for good.

As gut-wrenching difficult as it was, I shared what I'd done with Mike. He said he forgave me but began pulling further away. I poured myself into reading my Bible and my new job as the assistant director of a new daycare. I rediscovered my relationship with God. He was the only one that could handle me. *How could I have forgotten that? How did I fall so far? When did I stop trusting Him and start trusting myself or someone else to fill that void?*

I'd created an absolute mess.

The guard's voice snapped me back to reality. I'd get a fifteen-minute call. I called Grandma and hoped to talk to Mike. She hadn't seen him; in fact, no one had. He wandered off after my sentencing. Soon, the line went dead. *Had it already been fifteen minutes?* The words, "Try the phone again," popped into my mind. It was a weird thought, but what did I have to lose?

I dialed Mike's mom, Cheryl. It rang and went through! I felt my lungs expand. It felt like mere moments when the phone shut off. "Please," was my prayer as I punched in the numbers. It rang through again. It was an absolute miracle and my lifeline. We cried together over the devastation of the worst-case scenario playing out. Cheryl did her best to encourage me. My former date walked by, so I hung up the phone in fear I'd get in trouble. He said, "Your grandma called and said you were cold. Here's a blanket."

I somehow managed to fall asleep that first night locked up. I awoke in a daze and wondered, *Where am I?* Reality set in as I looked around and sighed. Shortly after, I was served what I believe was breakfast and told I'd leave for prison soon. Mike was on his way to visit before I left. I stared down at my orange and white jumpsuit. *I'd better get used to looking like this.*

I paced until Mike arrived. Relief fell from my body as I saw him on the other side of a plexiglass wall. I longed to touch him, but sat and picked up the phone instead. Mike did his best to appear calm and collected, but his eyes revealed a different story. He was scared. We weren't prepared for this. No one had answers about what prison was like. In fact, when they told me I was going to York, I thought they said "New York."

"The prison is two hours away, but it's better than states away," Mike said.

He brought the only things I could take with me: my glasses and his Bible. The time quickly escaped. I had no idea when I'd see him again. My heart broke as I thought about how we'd just started healing our fragile marriage.

When it was time to leave, an officer cuffed and escorted me outside. He said, "We have the same last name; I wonder if we're related?"

I slumped into the back seat and told him it was my husband's last name. There was a female officer to keep in conversation with him. My mind wandered as we drove through my hometown for the last time.

I was invited to Vacation Bible School when I was ten. I sat on freshly cut green grass and heard God loved me so much that He sent His Son to die for me. The teacher said I could ask Him into my heart and life. "Alone" was something I knew well. I desperately wanted what this teacher was selling. I proudly plead my allegiance with my right hand raised for all to see. The table full of cookies and watered-down

Kool-Aid in the gravel parking lot behind me disappeared, and a new presence was felt. I was covered. Jesus had my back. And I'd definitely need Him.

It doesn't make sense I'd attend church every time the doors were open. I rode the school bus for two hours every day and then hit the church bus every chance I could. I was a bus kid, hands down. Eventually, I felt like church was family. I looked up to them and their nicely tucked families in pews.

I followed the youth to camp in the Rockies. I felt peace, unlike anything I'd experienced. I entered this serene silence and heard God say He had an amazing plan for my life. On the last day, we circled around the campfire and threw a stick in the fire, signifying that we surrendered our lives to Him. I felt a call to missions or teaching.

With excitement, I exploded to my parents: I was sold out for Jesus. My dad wasn't excited. In fact, he thought I'd joined a cult and said I couldn't go back to church.

I ran to my bed and collapsed. I had wanted to share with my parents and now felt a great chasm between us. I looked at a picture of my family, thinking, "I'm the only one in this picture who believes in God." As I stared, I felt led to look behind the picture. There was a paper behind it saying, "Only one life, 'twill soon be passed; only what's done for Christ will last." It was the words my heart needed to hear. It didn't matter what I went through. The only thing that mattered was what I did for Christ.

My mission was to be the perfect kid, so my parents would accept Christ. I'd heard our sin affects others. Whenever I sinned, I confessed and prayed that my consequences would fall and stop with me. I didn't want anyone else to take the fall. I worked diligently, gained acceptance, sought approval, and served the church.

My best friend headed to Florida to the only college my church endorsed. I desperately wanted to attend a Christian college. My parents would only allow me to go if my bestie was there. This ideal life in Florida excited me to no end. I applied for scholarships despite the requirements for instate accredited colleges. This college was out of state and unaccredited. It was a miracle I received three scholarships that all waived their requirements. I was grounded by the reality I'd be leaving my sisters. They went everywhere with me.

The first time I heard my teacher pray, I felt at home. My teacher was a seasoned believer, and I loved his class. I'd get lost in his Southern heart for God. After a week, he asked me to stay after class. I nervously waited. With kind eyes, he said I was struggling. I was dumbfounded. Our lecture class was huge. This man of God must know something I didn't. I then remembered things at home were spiraling out of control. I tried to formulate the words for a man I hardly knew about how I desperately wanted my parents to accept Christ. Suddenly, a floodgate of emotion flowed, and I expressed my heart for my parents.

He shared the story about the jailer who received Christ and told his family. His family received Christ because of the jailer's faith. My teacher said he couldn't promise my parents would accept Christ, but God hears and honors big hearts for others. He stood in the gap and prayed with me. He demonstrated much that day. He peered into his class and sensed that I needed something. God knew my pain, and He saw me.

I was beyond excited when both my parents accepted Jesus that summer. They still battled with years of mental, emotional, and various abuse, but they'd invited Jesus into their mess. Their daughter was leaving, but Jesus would remain.

—o—o—c

We pulled up to the prison gates. Brick walls and coiled razor-wire fencing surrounded the prison. The doors opened, and we pulled through. I looked behind me and stared at the doors. I silently begged them not to shut. The doors didn't heed my plea and quickly cut me off from the outside world. I was now in prison.

CHAPTER 2

Segregation

I was escorted into a brick "Intake" building. It contained several showers and an office. A guard told me to strip, shower, and put a delouse liquid on my hair. I sat on the bench, shivering under a thin, ratty coverup, waiting for the treatment to finish.

I dressed in gray khakis and met the caseworker. After formalities, she said "Segregation" was best for me. I'd never heard any prison terms, so I had no idea where I was going. Segregation means the "isolation unit," often called the "pit" or "hole." New inmates never go to Segregation, but that's where I was headed. I walked down a long metal-encased hall with doors slamming behind me as I passed until I arrived at a metal room. Inside was a metal bed, toilet, and sink. There were tiny holes in the thick metal door that I'd attempt to speak through, but the guards struggled to hear me with their ears pressed to the door.

Let us brave prison together. We'll unfold the days I penned, crayoned at first, when I was locked up. We start in the heart of prison itself. Segregation means "the setting apart of a person from the main body," ironically, the story of my life. Enter the small metal box, echoing the faintest of sounds. My prayer is we hear something extraordinary from the heart of God.

September 30, 2007

I miss you more with every passing day. I know God has a reason for me being in the Segregation Unit, but I wish I knew why. It's difficult to talk to or understand anyone in my cell. The first person I met was Tinley, across from me. If I press my ear against the door, I can hear her. She said when she saw me, she thought, "Why are they bringing Little House on the Prairie to Segregation?" I had to laugh. She believes she's down here to get her focus on God. She has anger issues. I told her it's difficult to swallow our pride when others are being hurtful. The hardest thing to do is walk away. That's what Jesus did, and He was innocent. He could've blown them away with one breath, but He said nothing.

I looked out my tiny window. It's starting to sprinkle. I wish I were outside twirling in it. I never took the time to dance in the rain when I was free. Remind me to always stop and dance in the rain, no matter how busy I get.

The caseworker said my only available program is at the Lincoln Regional Center (LRC), but they have to interview me. Depending on their evaluation, I may have to go there and complete treatment. It's a mental hospital that has sex offender programming for female inmates.

I know God's in control, but He's done everything I prayed He wouldn't. I trust Him, but I'm scared. Fear and trust are on opposite sides. That hospital cannot be where God wants me, but I've been wrong all along. I'm trying to be content wherever God puts me. I think I'm content, but then I get afraid of the unknown ahead. God is trying me, and I want to come out of this pit as gold. I know God goes with me, but no actual person goes with me. I go alone.

I don't feel I'm accomplishing anything. I just sit here all day. God promises to use everything for good. I'm thankful for your Bible. I'd be lost without it. I feel like I'm literally living out the book of Psalms. My mind is exhausted from trying to keep myself busy all day. I read and pray all day. I hope to call you tomorrow.

September 31, 2007

One of my five privileges is walking outside in a tiny fenced-in box. There are three chained boxes next to each other. I walk down the hall with doors slamming behind me as I go. I have a great desire to talk to someone, and God heard. My name was called, along with two others.

They were already in their boxes talking, so I just listened. I kinda wish I hadn't. I kept praying about what I should say. Finally, one woman asked my name. She said, "I knew you were a Christian. When you walked outside, you had this glow around you and seemed pure." Cami shared her struggle of re-offending to come back to prison, where her girlfriend has a life sentence.

It doesn't make sense; Cami continues to live in prison when there's real life on the other side. She knows she's trapped and is making horrible decisions. That's what happens when something enslaves you. Satan is the father of confusion. You see life, but it's veiled death. And I can relate to that. I encouraged her to do what was right and get back to her children. It felt incredible that God used me to speak. Pray I never lose my "glow" for Him.

Mail comes at night and greatly helps with the homesickness that hits at bedtime. Believers' words are spiritual food that strengthens and sustains me, like manna from heaven. Please thank them and ask them not to stop until I'm out of here.

It's detrimental I stay in God's light and state of mind. Misery loves company, and there's plenty here and more on the yard. It's Satan's playground, and he's having one heck of a party.

October 1, 2007

New inmates go to D&E [Diagnostic and Evaluation]. They learn procedures like filling out paperwork requests, visitation, phone, Canteen, and rules—a month-long prison boot camp on how to survive prison.

I'm attempting to fill out paperwork. It took me a while to understand what "Go fly a kite" meant. A kite is a form you have to fill out for everything. I only had a crayon, so I had to "kite" request a pen. I received it, but it's a short white stick.

I only get one phone call per week rather than one per day, like D&E. The mere fifteen minutes a day isn't enough, but once a week is torture. I don't even know what time slot I'll get and if you'll be at work. I miss your voice!

If you get approval to visit while I'm in Segregation, brace yourself. I'll be fully shackled. While in Segregation, I'm fully shackled anytime I leave my cage. I leave daily to see doctors and take tests.

I just met with the mental health doctor. I'll have to take that 600-question sexual test the probation office made me take before sentencing. The wording of those questions is disgusting and insane. My lawyer said the Pope himself would fail because they'd think he's lying.

She continued sucking the wind from my sails by saying it's rare for a sex offender to go to Work Release; I should shift my focus to being in prison or the hospital. Sex offenders rarely get first-eligible parol, so I should expect my release in four years, rather than two. I felt my heart bottom out. Looking at that date completely overwhelms me. No one ever said I'd have to do the full four years! If I qualify for the hospital, I'll be there for two years. That's how long the fastest person completed it.

I miss you and everyone terribly. Please give my address to anyone who wants to write. I need to hear your voice. I miss life itself. Tell everyone all our letters are read through. I hope our paperwork gets cleared soon. Pray, baby, pray.

October 2, 2007

I keep receiving papers describing how they view my crime, the amount of time, and how the law perceives it. It's extremely heavy and nauseating. I'm sick that I'll be labeled as a sex offender. Everyone will see me as a monster. Colossians 2:14, "Blotting out the handwriting of the ordinances [old arrest warrant] that was against us, which was contrary to us, and took it out of the way, nailing it to his cross." I'm physically laying these papers down and asking God to nail them to the cross of Christ. He died for my sin.

I'm asking God for wisdom, insight, and life-giving words. I'm learning all I can from God while I'm here. That's probably why I'm in Segregation. I've time alone to read, pray, and prepare myself. Although, I'll never be truly ready for what's to come. I can reach women here I'd never been able to reach. Most of them have been here for years.

When I was outside with Cami, she asked me several questions. I could barely see her face through the chains, but she smiled and said, "Nobody ever explained it just like you did." I want to feel like that every day, that I truly helped someone. That brings more joy than anything else. To help them see God's light come on.

A friend gave me a challenge. She asked me to pick a verb that I wanted to be—a word to summarize myself and express in life. I chose "love." I felt rejected by our church, Christians, and society.

After everything happened, I prayed I'd love others no matter what they've done.

It kind of makes sense why God would allow me to go to prison. I basically asked God to send me here. I told God I'd do whatever He wanted me to do, and go wherever He wanted me to go. The cherry on top of my sacrificial sundae is, I told God to let me love others going through the same thing I'm going through. I was the only one that had a chance to love these women. I think I sealed the deal without knowing it. I think God just revealed why I'm here, and it's quite the revelation.

I wish it could be different and that I could see you. God will take care of us and our marriage. When we're obedient and honor Him in the struggle, we'll reap blessings. We'll get through this, and draw closer to God and each other, despite the razor fencing separating us. I'm overwhelmed that God showed me why I'm here: to show His love, true love, to others.

These women are broken and need love. Pray they see Christ's love through me and the joy of being a Christian while I'm living among them. It's not a ministry that comes in once a week. I'm here *with* them. Prison is a very scary place and feels very dark. I need prayer and protection daily. I've no strength of my own and need encouragement. Remind me when it gets tough that I'm here to love others. Read this to my family so they don't worry as much. Thank you for sharing my letters to save me from hand cramps.

Thankfully, the day is winding down. I'm staring at a picture of us. What a long monster roller coaster this year has been. I'm thankful you've stayed with me for the ride. I don't want to imagine life without you. I'm encouraged by what we've already overcome. I pray we draw closer to God and become less of ourselves and more like Christ. It's your gentle and encouraging voice I hear telling me to keep going when it gets hard.

I often wake up at night when the big metal doors slam open and shut at guard checks. The guard comes every hour, and my room is next to a set of doors. I jolt awake, all out of sorts. I often think I'm having the worst dream of my life. Then I look around and realize where I am. Panic shoots through my core as I again remember I'm alone. I quote Psalm 57:1, "Be merciful unto me, O God, be merciful to me! For my soul trusts in You; And in the shadow of Your wings I will make my refuge, until these calamities have passed by."

I daydream during these difficult moments of something you once said. You said we could take a second honeymoon to the ocean. I imagine us on the beach, although I don't know if I'll be allowed to travel. But I dream, and let myself go. I'm completely free on the inside and out. I breathe in fresh sea salt air and watch the beautiful sunset over the tide as you hold me in your arms. It helps ease the pain inside.

October 3, 2007

This morning I awoke to a screaming woman who was just brought in. I'd better get used to this. I learned I'm going to North Hall once I hit the yard. It's the unit for violent offenders. Since my charge is "attempted assault," I'll be with the most violent women in prison. Living with violent women doesn't sound appealing, especially after hearing this woman explode all morning.

My Canteen came! I never liked Snickers before, but it was a sight for sore eyes. I got envelopes so I can send letters out. I just smashed that Snickers. Everyone says you gain weight here. I'm guessing it's because they buy food from Canteen.

October 4, 2007

I took a test for job placement and filled out a career plan for when I'm released. I said I want to be a housewife or bakery manager. It's difficult thinking I can't teach again. I spent four years working toward something I'll never do again. It's extremely heavy, so I try not to think about it.

Speaking of heavy, I had to be fully shackled again today. I'm stripped and shackled each time I leave. The handcuffs are attached to a chain around my waist. Another chain leads to my feet, which are also cuffed. The ankle cuffs are the worst as they dig into my ankles, making walking difficult and painful. I'm the most chained inmate because I'm new and in Segregation.

I just got back from my physical. Though I'd just gotten back from the eye doctor, I was stripped, shackled, and violated all over again. My ankles are bleeding, making each step a nightmare. The pain is nothing compared to how I feel inside. These chains define me. I'm a monster. Everyone on the yard stops and stares at me. No one knows who I am or why I'm in Segregation. Today a woman yelled at me, "Fresh meat, tasty treat!"

I talked to the officers that escorted me. They asked why I am here. "Shouldn't you know?" I thought. They said I'm too nice to go through all this. They seemed puzzled about why I was in Segregation. It's the same questions on each shackled-up trip.

Once I got to my physical, I was stripped again, taking my clothes off more times than I can count. Knowing my luck, I'll go to the dentist later and spend another hour getting suited up. I'm glad I'm getting this done so I can hit the yard, but come on. Why can't we make appointments at the same time? Less work for everyone.

I received more evaluations. It wasn't too bad, but I hate trick questions. One was, "I take all my responsibilities seriously." Well, obviously, I didn't, but I'm a responsible person overall. How can that be true/false? No one is perfect all the time.

If you ever find out what these women are here for, don't tell me. I see them looking and whispering about me. I want to be kind and full of grace and love. As 1 John 4:18 says, "There is no fear in love, but perfect love casteth out fear, because fear hath torment. He that fears is not made perfect in love." I won't fear these women if I love them. I don't want to be tormented by fear, which is easy here.

I thought our Visiting Day was Sunday, but it's Saturday. I can't call you because my phone sheet was wrong. You're going to drive two hours just to drive back without seeing me. I sent the Warden a kite. I thought I had Segregation visitation, but I'm D&E since that's where I'm supposed to be. The guards don't even know. I can't call or see you, and I'm supposed to do both.

There's nothing I can do. Worrying about you upsets me, and then I have a bad attitude and want to give up. I can't allow myself to feel that way. Being here is difficult enough without desperation rearing its ugly head. I gave it to God and asked Him to help you figure it out. I'm sorry I filled the form out wrong. I should be in D&E, where I learn everything. Here, I attempt to communicate through a metal door by sending forms and waiting days for a response. I keep throwing my worry at His feet.

You asked me what I can do here. I get five privileges a week. The first is the book cart that gets wheeled by daily. There's a slot on the outside of my door. The guard pulls down the slot, and I try to reach out and find a book. The second is taking a shower three times a week at the end of the hall. The guards clear the hall, lock their station, and then my door unlocks. I walk to the shower and get locked in.

The third is using the razor in the shower. It shouldn't be a privilege because it doesn't cut hair, just pulls and rips it out. The fourth is going outside. I don't feel like I'm outside, except for getting

21

fresh air. The final privilege is cleaning my room. Yes, Mike, it's a privilege. Those are my goodies, so please don't be jealous.

The light stays on all night, so I hide under the covers. Med call is at 5:30 a.m., and breakfast is at 7. Guards check every thirty minutes and write down what they see, including me using the restroom.

I talked to the woman in the cell next to mine and shared the Gospel. Terry professes to be a believer, but practices Wicca. She said she's more of a conversationalist and loves nature. Terry seems nice, but something is off about her.

October 7, 2007

It's Visiting in Segregation. I've seen women come and go. It's probably good you didn't come. I think you'd be scared, seeing me chained up. It'll be better when I'm on the yard. You should sell my car and cell phone. It feels like I'll be dead for the next few years.

I keep thinking about why I'm here. I hate what I did and how I hurt others. I know God has separated my sin as far as the East is from the West and remembers it no more. I know I must pay for what I've done, but shame sweeps over me. I feel like God's still mad and punishing me more than He does others. And if that's true, why do I have a deep knowledge of Him and sense His ministry here in this prison? Why would I feel led to share what He tells me? I hate thinking of failing Him again. He's enough, and all I have. Pray these doubts flee.

I got a letter from my dad. This is truly a precious gift, as he's never written to me. He's struggling with the fact that I'm here. I hope he's encouraging himself in the Word. I don't know how else a father gets through seeing their daughter in prison. Would you please visit him once in a while? I know I ask much of you, but I can't do these things myself. I'm sure he's angry, but underneath, he's just hurting.

One of my preschool parents wrote saying she doesn't see me how society does, but as a teacher whom her children adore. She cried for days after hearing I left and would endure all this. It means so much that she supports me despite the lies smeared all over the papers.

I save reading your letter for last. I'm relieved you heard you can't visit me from the Warden. I never know what they tell you. It drives me crazy that we cannot communicate through this. I feel sick going another week without seeing you, but I hated that you'd travel all that way without seeing me.

It's interesting that you mentioned our future children. I thought about that today. It's difficult that I won't see children for several years. I pray I can have children. As 1 Peter 5:10 says, "But the God of all grace, who has called us unto his eternal glory by Christ Jesus, after you have suffered a while, make you perfect, establish, strengthen, settle you."

October 9, 2007

Last night some women were singing, so I joined. They requested songs for me to sing. We sang for hours, and my heart needed that. Dinner was pizza with leftover toppings. Lunch was soup with peas, carrots, and lima beans. I've never eaten so many lima beans.

I just got back from Medical. There isn't any privacy with several people in the room. The nurse asked what my charge was, even though she had it on her form. When I said "attempted sexual assault," everyone stared at me.

I passed D&E on my way back. They talk to each other, play games, have calls and visits, and don't wear shackles. Why am I here? Why do I feel like a monster everywhere I go? What is the point of this?

I know God carries me through. I long for Him to sit on my bed and hold my shaking hands. I want to hear Him speak directly to my throbbing heart and tell me some sort of life-giving word. It feels like winter, and everything is frozen. Life has stopped, including my faintly beating heart. I'm writing with a dull crayon in the pit of a prison. Women here for bad behavior were released to the yard. Here I remain, wanting my pencil sharpened.

Tinley left, and a giant woman named Sasha replaced her. She just told me I was cute, to which I replied, "Thanks, my husband thinks so too."

October 10, 2007

I was assigned my caseworker. It's the same woman who put me into Segregation. Fear settled in, and I want to go home. My charge makes my life an absolute nightmare. Now I'm thinking of that hospital all over again. I don't want to go to a mental hospital. I'm scared and just want you. I haven't heard your voice in over two weeks.

I finally got my phone sheet back, but I'm only allowed one call the entire time I'm in Segregation. I'll save it until I know you can visit. The guard doesn't know when I get a visit or even who to kite about it. Everyone I kite belittles me because they assume I'm a discipline problem. I never get any answers. I can't handle it. I give this to God.

CHAPTER 3

Rise and Fall

October 11, 2007

After I turned in that frantic letter, my prayers were answered. A man came and said you can come Sunday morning. I'll try calling Saturday evening.

I'm sorry for the end of my letter. I pray God makes me more like Him and less of me. I need more faith and trust in Him. The only thing I can control is my walk with God. My circumstances get the best of me, and I panic. At the very end of that letter, I simply said, "I give it to Him." One minute later, the lieutenant came as an answer to my prayer. I don't like learning to walk by faith like this; it's not easy at all!

There's a minor in D&E. Someone hinted my charge could be why I'm not there. My sister's a teenager. I don't know if I'll get to visit her. It's possible I won't be able to hug you because of my charge. I can't imagine being a registered sex offender. How will it impact you, our possible children, and my family? It's like a hurricane brewing and building. I give it to God, but it's my constant overshadowing rain clouds, reminding me of what's to come.

I just read a letter from Pastor and the tears won't stop. I wrote him asking if I could write a letter to the church saying I was sorry and ask for forgiveness. You said you'd read it for me when you read yours. Pastor replied, "I do believe it'd be a step in the right direction. Go ahead and write something and express your heart for the people's attention."

Mike, perhaps I'm reading too much into this, but it sounds like he wants me to do more. This letter is just a step. I'm writing Todd's parents, the principal, and others I need to make amends with. Pastor knows that, so what else is there? Why is this letter not enough? What more can I give? My blood? I'm in prison! Segregation at that. I'll never see my childhood church again as they revoked my membership. I feel like I've disappointed him all over.

This letter has stirred everything up. My mind wanders to how it all went down.

A few months after I told you about Todd, you brought up the word "divorce." You shut down and were brutally mean to me. I felt awful, but desperate to show you I was still in this marriage. I spent more time with Charles's wife, Jackie. She wanted to hang out together all the time. I confided in Jackie about my affair, but that I was working on my relationship with you and God.

We then went to Illinois for your mom's birthday, and Jackie begged to come. It seemed like a nice distraction to our frigid marriage, so I agreed. In Illinois, your anger ignited. I hated what I had done but didn't know how to undo the damage.

One night, as I looked at the busy highway, I thought walking into that may be easier. I wanted the pain to be over. It freaked me out that I'd considered suicide, and I ran upstairs to Jackie, sobbing to her. She had a strange smile on her face as she stroked my head. I was unsettled, so I told you I wanted to leave Illinois. We abruptly left in the middle of the night. Jackie volunteered to sit in the front so I could lie down in the back. It felt off, so I said the front was fine.

I wanted to talk to Pastor, so we dropped Jackie off and knocked on Pastor's door in the middle of the night. He answered, and I poured out my affair. You sat like a stone statue next to me. Pastor asked if the person I had the affair with was in the church so he could deal with it. I was scared to involve anyone else and just wanted to work on our marriage. Pastor said we'd meet the next day.

The next day, you said I was on my own. I entered the church and discovered two deacons in the room, one being Charles's brother. Pastor sensed I was uneasy, but said he needed accountability. He continued that people speculated Todd was who I had the affair with. Before I could reply, he continued, saying he had checked into the law and Todd was of legal consent. I knew it was a huge sin, but I'd never seriously considered legal trouble. I told him it was Todd. Pastor said he'd get back to me, and I went home.

When I arrived, you were packing to move back to Illinois. Pastor called with news that sent my already chaotic life into a greater whirlwind. He'd received false information from Charles's brother. Todd was just shy of the age of consent. He gave me the name of a lawyer. I lifelessly hung up and called the lawyer. All I heard was it was serious, and I needed $10,000.

I was in a fog as I drove to my parents' house to share what their firstborn had done. I'd never been in trouble. They panicked and called my grandpa, who came right away. He said he'd figure it out and not worry about the money, but he wanted me to get away for a bit.

I never went to work the next morning. It was a new daycare, and I didn't want it to go down with me. Grandpa sent me to Vegas to visit my Uncle Ron, his son. I went through the motions as I said goodbye to you. I was losing my house, job, career, church, family, and most importantly, you. My lawyer said my punishment should be minimal, but anything could happen. How could I prepare for that?

Ron lived minutes away from the Las Vegas Strip. I felt like I experienced the aftermath of a midlife crisis in my twenties. I listened to Christian music to escape my demolished life. I went to nearby parks to run and sing until I was breathless.

You called after I'd arrived. It was basic business without mention of divorce. Then you began opening beyond the surface level. I felt a flicker of hope and wanted to feed this fire. Could you change your mind? Could we actually survive this? I now faced the law. Would you walk with me here? I desperately desired actual flesh to lean on. "God, protect my heart, guide me, and don't let me fixate on what could diminish again." You were guarded, but said you missed me. It felt so good, so familiar. You were my best friend.

Then I had a dream; I sat at a large wooden table with Pastor at the head. You and Jackie sat on opposite sides and played footsie with each other under the table. Stunned, I announced to everyone what you were doing.

The next day, I told you about this dream. You didn't say much then but called the following day. You had something to tell me and quickly stated, "I had an affair with Jackie." I couldn't process it and hung up the phone. I had to escape. I couldn't breathe. I ran outside with my phone still in hand. I wandered back and forth on the sidewalk. You called back, upset I'd hung up, and said, "I wasn't finished; she's pregnant and doesn't know who the father is."

Sharp knives pierced my heart. I hung up again. It was all I could do to disengage. Since Pastor was at the head of the table in my dream, I felt like I should call him, but I was scared. Grandpa was upset with Pastor for allowing deacons in the room when I shared in confidence. One deacon leaked, and the news spread like wildfire throughout our church. Jackie's face popped into my mind. How could she do that after everything I did for her? I let her in, shared what Charles did, brought her on vacation, and trusted her. While I tried to protect her marriage, she stabbed me in the back. I know I had an affair too, but this felt personal on many levels.

I called Pastor and told him everything. He wanted to tell Charles as he'd been counseling him. Charles wasn't doing well. *Join the club, Charles.* Pastor said to wait on God. I was a little disappointed that was all he said. God had already told me that morning, "Be still and know that I am God."

Broken pieces lay in every direction I looked. I didn't want to give up on you, but I was devastated. I hurt Todd and his family, the church, the school, and my family, and I ended my teaching career. I failed everyone at some level. I didn't want to fail one more thing. I heard God say, "Run to Me; I've never failed you or forsaken you. You can trust Me."

Slowly, we started talking again. Something had changed. You wanted our marriage to work. On the other hand, I wanted to run. You were adamant that I fly to Illinois and leave Vegas, but I didn't want to go. Your parents knew everything. The last time I was there, Jackie was with us. Her lies and twisted smile came into my mind. She spent time with Cheryl. Why did she have to poison another thing?

I finally consented to leave. Your first comment was you didn't recognize me because I'd lost weight. I'm certain my smile hibernated as well. The next month, we tried to communicate. I felt betrayed, shut down, and didn't trust you. I knew what I'd done was the same sin, but yours felt more personal. It ran deeper; she was my best friend.

You wanted to be intimate. You said it was the last time with her, and you wanted it gone forever. I felt every door in my mind, heart, and body close down. How could I be intimate with you after this? I felt alone in a cave with only a ray of light peering in. God softened my heart as I tried to hear your brokenness. I vowed to love you through anything. I told God I was doing it for Him. That's the only way I got through that first time. As I began giving myself little by little to you, I felt the healing process begin. I didn't yet like you, but I had vowed to love you.

October 12, 2007

My heart breaks as I read your letter. Don't feel worthless or helpless. You're doing everything you can. You write every day, keep everyone updated, send money, pray, and continue growing closer to God. Put me into God's hands. He won't drop me. We've come so far and are fiercely fighting for our marriage.

I'm reading in Hosea where he stays with his wife after she betrayed him with other men. God compares her with the children of Israel. God still wants, loves, and comforts her. Hosea buys her back. What love! I feel God talking to us in Hosea 14:4: "Then I will heal you of your faithlessness; my love will know no bounds, for my anger will be gone forever."

Could you type a weekly letter so you're not always updating everyone? Once I hit the yard, I'll have a job and won't be able to write as much. Please keep all my letters. Who knows, maybe we can turn them into something someday.

October 13, 2007

I talked to you! It'd been three weeks, and I desperately missed your voice. It carried me away from this cold, metal cage. It was like coming up for air after holding my breath underwater for too long. I couldn't talk fast enough. Your calming voice eases the harsh surroundings like a lullaby. I will see you tomorrow! I'm never going to fall asleep.

I've been thinking about teaching. I know I can't teach in a school, but that doesn't mean I can't be a teacher of a different kind. God gives spiritual gifts, and they don't go away. In his repentance in Psalm 51:13, David says, "Then I will teach transgressors thy ways; and sinners shall be converted unto thee." A missionary takes the Gospel to the lost. That's my goal, and I shouldn't care what others say or think. The only thing that matters is pleasing God.

October 14, 2007

I just got back from my visit with you and my parents. What a balm to my aching heart. I felt a rush of comfort looking into your eyes. I didn't want to let go of our brief hug. It was challenging with my parents there, but I'm glad they came.

I know my dad can be a lot to take in, but think about how scared he is. There's nothing he can do to help his little girl. He doesn't handle things as well as you. I thought he was going to throw up when he first saw me all shackled up. I wrote a little poem about how I felt with our time together.

"Visitation"

A breath of fresh air to see your face,
You draw me close in your loving embrace.
Hold me close; please never let go,
The desire to rest in your arms is all I know.

As we sit, you quickly reach for my hand,
It reassures me why you are my man.
Your strong, comforting words bring me to tears,
Reminds my aching heart of our upcoming years.

I stare into depths of blue; I see your soul,
Myself reflecting in you; for once, I am whole.
Your gaze fixed on me; I see love afire,
To remember your face is my heart's true desire.

We talk of things in your life and mine,
My mind drifts to complete reunion and long for that time.
You help me regain focus for tasks ahead,
I must forsake doubt and fear, and trust God instead.

I sigh as our departure draws so very near,
You express your love and purpose of why I'm here.
We bow our hearts before our God and King,
We pray for strength in the journey; we give Him everything.

My heart begins to miss you, long before you're gone,
You remind me of our next visit and urge me to stay strong.
We rise to our feet and give our last goodbye,
One last embrace, my heart breathes the longest sigh.

I watch you leave this awful place, and yet I must remain,
My heart breaks watching you walk away, for without you, I'm not the same.
I know one sweet day, I will finally be free,
Until then, may the Lord be between you and me.

Watching you walk away was the most difficult thing I didn't anticipate. You walked through the metal locked gates, razor wire, and this awful place. You went home without me. Somewhere this deep pain welled up inside, escaped and choked me. I try my best to push it away, because I don't know what to do with it.

You asked me about my dreams for the future, so I think about that instead. I want you to have a job that provides. I'll be a stay-at-home mom to three beautiful children and actively involved in ministry. I'll be a cake decorator on the side. We won't live in Nebraska. I guess it depends on where we can live. I'd love to live in Florida. I want to have land for our two dogs and puppies on the way. I'll hold a baby in my arms within two years of being out.

October 15, 2007

Last night was rough. Terry talked to a female guard about the things they do sexually with women. They used the most graphic language

I've ever heard. I felt sick and unsettled afterward, especially since this was the guard on duty.

Brace yourself. I hate telling you any of this because I don't want to worry you, but know I'm on the other side of it. I fell in the shower and lost consciousness. I was trying to shave with the ridiculous razor that refuses to cut hair. There isn't much control over the water temperature, and it gets really hot. I didn't realize there was a metal vent. Mine was shut.

I bent over, attempting to cut the hair, and started blacking out. I stopped and waited. My vision cleared, so I tried again. Then it happened again, longer, and more intense. I started feeling faint. I grabbed the arm rail and tried to get out of the shower. I felt myself fading away. I hit my head on the concrete floor and fumbled in the dark. I could feel, but couldn't see. I crawled around, trying to find my clothes, and ran into the walls. It was the same guard that talked with Terry, so I tried to get dressed.

The inmate in the shower next to me got the guard to come. I had to be strip-searched and shackled to go to Medical. My head and neck were throbbing. I could hardly move. Medical gave me Tylenol and said I strained my neck. My neck hurts more than my head. I can't believe I lost consciousness. I remember praying throughout the whole thing. I definitely won't be shaving again.

October 16, 2007

I received my beloved mail, including a letter from you. I hang heavier than usual. I forget details of your face and long to remember. You wrote I should share my struggles and not hold back. I'm staring down this endless tunnel of time, and it creates this ball of heaviness inside. I know God gives me strength, but staying strong for so long makes me cry. Sometimes I'm okay, but when something else happens, I collapse.

My body is really sore and keeps me up at night. These heartfelt letters encourage me to keep my chin up, but my chin is not up tonight. Keeping your chin up for years isn't an easy task. It'll have to become who I am. I don't know how God thinks I can do this on my own. I wish I had someone to shoulder this journey with me. I feel tried by fire that burns to my core. I know with Christ I can do this. I need to read my Bible.

I was scared to go back in the shower. This time, I opened the vent. The guard said he can't see in, which is a complete lie. But I'd rather be seen naked than pass out on the floor again. Being in a metal shower box with all that steam is horrendous, especially when you're locked in.

This afternoon, I looked out my metal window and saw a butterfly land on the tiny ledge. It was so close that I could make out its fragile details. As it fluttered, I breathed deeply, as if trying to receive its freeing life. This was the first of any kind of nature I'd seen while being in the pit. God sent this butterfly just for me.

A guard just told me to pack my clothes up. I'm feverishly writing in a lame attempt to settle my nerves. I can't believe I'm hitting the yard. I don't have to wear the shackles and can just walk out of here. I'm scared, but ready. Here goes nothing.

CHAPTER 4

North Hall

October 17, 2017

I'm finally out of Segregation. North Hall is the building for violent offenders. It contains four halls that meet in the center with a dayroom, four telephones, and guard control, "the bubble." Hall A and B are where the most violent inmates are housed. Almost all of them committed murder. Guess where yours truly is housed? Yep, I'm in A. I live with the most dangerous women in the state.

I met both my cellmates. Daisy is my age and also just hit the yard. Nicole's 36 and has been here a while. Nicole acts like she's in charge of the cell and runs a tight ship. I'm assigned the top bunk over Nicole. Our cell is tiny, with the toilet in our room open for all to see.

My cellmates told me of a few inmates to steer clear of. One of them is Sasha, who lives down my hall. Sasha's in several violent love triangles. She was across from me in Segregation and tried to hit on me. Another inmate I was warned about was Terry. Terry was next to me in Segregation and isn't out yet. Terry has a life sentence for decapitating someone. She's a transfer from another state.

It's easy to be written up. I can't get an MR [misconduct report] if I want a chance at Work Release. There are several unwritten rules I need to learn. Room doors unlock at 6 a.m. We have a lockdown from 4:30 to 6 p.m, with dinner following based on our hall. Evening lockdown is at 8:30 p.m. every night, with doors locked until the next day.

When money gets sent in, it goes into my account called "Books." I fill out request forms for Canteen. We only get fifteen minutes per day of phone time and have to buy it. There are only four phones for the 150 women, so there's always a line to talk.

I tried calling you, but you weren't there. You don't even know I hit the yard today. I got ahold of my dad and he'll let you know. I'm looking through my checkered metal window and see a field of grazing cows in the rain. The picture of our vacation at the Dells hangs by my window. That vacation was unlike any vacation I'd ever experienced, or ever will.

We had only a short month in Illinois, learning how to communicate with each other and begin healing. We worked together, fixing up houses while fixing the holes in our marriage. My family had planned a trip to the Dells, and I really wanted to go. I missed my sisters, as I felt closer to them than just a sister growing up. They were five and nine years younger, and I took care of them for much of their lives.

On our last day, we took old-fashioned photos. My sisters went with the "Outlaw" theme, complete with a "Wanted" sign above. Ironically, that was the day a nationwide warrant went out for my arrest. Since I wasn't home, they thought I was fleeing the country. My parents asked you to deliver the news.

I was in the hotel room, standing between two beds with a sister on each bed. As you told me about the warrant, you positioned yourself between me and the balcony. I lifelessly walked toward you, fixed my gaze on the sliding glass window, and peered out. My name was broadcasted all over the country, and soon everyone would know. I looked at each terrified sister, drained of color. I'd have to continue for them. I couldn't jump; I couldn't do that to them or you.

October 18, 2007

I got up early to read my Bible. Nicole has her TV on with the volume cranked up constantly, which is very distracting. She said we can't have another TV in our cell. TVs are expensive anyway, and I need shoes. I was issued extremely uncomfortable, stiff black combat boots. I can order a pair of walking shoes from the catalog as well as a pair of jeans and a tee shirt. I haven't received my state-issued clothes from Property. I literally only have the clothes on my back.

I saw my caseworker and received my job assignment. I'll be a "Teacher's Aide," making $2 a day. She explained after a year and 35 points, I may qualify for Work Release. I have 32 points. I accumulate points by working and completing my programming. My only program is LRC, pending evaluation. I would've been closer, but my criminal charge killed me, as well as being a young offender and the length of my sentence.

I started at the school today and stepped into pure chaos. There are only two classrooms for all the inmates that need their GED. Two paid teachers from the "outs" come in. There are desks shoved everywhere in an attempt to accommodate everyone. There are two a.m. and two p.m. classes.

I walked down the cramped aisle and received a slap on my butt. I turned around to discover three women cramped around me. All appeared to be working. I had no idea what to do. I pretended like it didn't happen and kept walking. Welcome to prison school. All but one of the other ten TAs live in the other housing unit. B bay is the unit for nonviolent women of lesser crimes.

Terry's out of Segregation and lives across the hall. She had opened up when we were in Segregation, but on the yard, she responds differently. She feeds off the women around her, and her demeanor changes. I'm taking advice and steering clear of her.

Tonight I was headed into the door of the dining hall when I stepped on the shoestring of the woman in front of me. One good step on such a tiny string sent the giant-sized woman flying into the air. I panicked when I saw Sasha sprawling onto her face in front of everyone. She's a good five inches taller and a hundred pounds heavier than I am. I endlessly apologized. She looked shocked and walked away. I cannot believe I did that! And of all people, Sasha! Lord, please help me not to send another violent convict flying into the air. *Welcome to the pen!*

October 19, 2007

It'll cost $15 a week for phone cards for the mere fifteen minutes a day, and $10 a week for envelopes. That alone is more than I make in a month. I don't know how anyone can make it without outside help. I also don't know why it's taking so long to get my clothing. I'll have to shower and put the same clothes back on.

Daisy said she's writing to her foster mom about wanting a relationship with God. Her mom's been praying Daisy would accept Jesus and meet someone who could show her how. Daisy said I'm the nicest girl she's ever met and that I shouldn't be in prison. She's convinced God put me in the worst place, on this hall, and in her cell just for her. Tears welled in my eyes when she spoke. We're going to do a Bible study together.

Daisy and I sat with a woman at dinner who asked who our other cellmate was. She said Nicole is extremely controlling and overbearing. Nicole's previous roommate freaked out on her and is in Segregation. It really rattled up Daisy.

I finally got my clothes, but they had the wrong inmate number stamped, so I have to return them. I just read your letter, and you said you're struggling with not seeing me. I'm struggling too. It's the worst at night.

October 20, 2007

I don't understand why I can't get your number to work. I want to talk to you. Daisy and I are doing a study. We hoped Nicole would join or at least allow us to have it in our cell, but she refuses. She's very moody. One minute she's fine, and the next, she's angry and demanding. I asked if she'd turn off her TV one hour a week for us to do our study. She said she doesn't do that. She's a cleaner and works only twenty minutes a day. She's always in our room watching TV. I'm trying to be kind and flexible, but this isn't your typical college roommate situation. I plan on walking outside as much as I can.

There's a sand volleyball court with women playing, so I jumped in. My teammates asked if I played "on the streets." I'm still not used to prison lingo. Then they asked why I was in prison and came from Segregation. I kindly said I just wanted to play volleyball. One woman said, "Don't worry, I'll find out."

These women will assume the worst and twist it however they want. They crave dirt in hopes of feeling better about whatever they did. I'd rather they hear it from me instead of the lies in the newspaper, but I feel like I'm supposed to be silent. I want to share

Jesus, but I wrestle as women keep asking questions about why I'm here. I have to be careful who I build conversations with.

Saturday nights, we don't receive mail. I miss hearing from you. Tomorrow I finally get to go to church. Daisy said she'd go, but she has to attend the other service. I wish I didn't have to go alone, but I am used to it. It reminds me of going alone as a child. Goodnight, my love.

October 21, 2007

Sunday

It's Church Day! I'm making verse cards to kill time. I write verses on 3x5 cards and memorize them as I walk around the yard. There's so much evil and heaviness in here. It brings peace to read the Word as I encircle the prison. It reminds me of college, when I prayed for someone on each lap I walked for PE. I look forward to getting a CD player, but it'll take a month. I desperately need uplifting music as I walk.

John 8:29 says, "And He that sent me is with me: the Father hath not left me alone; for I always do those things that please him." I need to receive that. It lifts the pressure off me about what happens here. I pray these women come to Christ and turn their lives around, but it's in God's control and timing. All I can do is obey Him and be ready to speak as the Holy Spirit prompts me.

I just got back from church. It started with the inmate choir rapping. One inmate sang, and the rest joined whenever they wanted. I think I just signed up to join that choir. I wonder if I can decline.

The message was good. She shared Romans 8:11, "But if the Spirit of Him that raised up Jesus from the dead dwells in you, he that raised up Christ from the dead shall also quicken your mortal bodies by his Spirit that dwells in you." We have such an awesome power living in us!

She also shared how, in Acts 16:23–34, God opened the jail doors. There was a huge chance I wouldn't get jail time, but I did. I got an extremely heavy load, but God could've rescued me any time. He has a purpose in my affliction. It's showing others how to overcome hurt and brokenness with the power of an Almighty God. To let others see the light inside me.

I talked to my mom. She's struggling with the unfairness of my sentence. I understand, but it's difficult for me to talk about. Life isn't fair, and apparently, God wants me in prison for a reason. I can't listen to negativity about what happened. Believe me; I know! I'm the one locked up.

Daisy was next to me, talking to her children. I can't imagine having children while being here. Her feet are covered in blisters from these horrible boots we wear. Somehow she and I were issued different boots that are horrendous. I tried encouraging her, but she's still crying.

Back in our room, I'd received several letters. When I looked at Daisy, her face fell. She didn't get a single letter. She asked to see the cards that people had sent me. I showed her everything, and she wrote down all the sayings in them. I gave her all the little things people had added, like bookmarks and verses. I'll ask your mom if someone in her prayer group would write to her.

I got a letter with money from some man asking if I'll write him. I don't want to be ungrateful, but I have no idea who this is. The director of the daycare wrote. She said she misses how I picked up her spirits and helped her see things clearly. She often invited me into her office to talk. I'd answer her questions about church, the Bible, and God. I miss those talks too.

Luke 7 spoke volumes as I read the story of the sinful woman. Jesus says, "You did not give me a kiss, but this woman, from the time I entered, has not stopped kissing my feet. You did not put oil on my head, but she has poured perfume on my feet. Therefore, I tell you, her many sins have been forgiven, FOR SHE LOVED MUCH. But he who has been forgiven little, loves little."

The more we grasp how our sin cut our Savior, the more we love the One who bled for us. We understand forgiveness on a deeper level. I can't judge someone for what they've done. I'm equally guilty. I pray God takes this lump of clay heart of mine and molds it into something beautiful for Him. I want to love someone no matter what. For truly, love covers a multitude of sins.

October 23, 2007

A guard just said I should've been able to have a visit last weekend. Immediate family can visit after D&E while the paperwork clears. I guess because I came from Segregation, no one told me. I would've loved to have seen you.

Could you find a picture of Grandpa? The only face wash they carry is Noxzema, and that's what Grandpa used. It has a distinct medicated smell. When I opened it up, all the memories came flooding back.

I was at my parents' house, bawling in my sister's bed. I told them what I'd done, how things went when I talked to Pastor, Mike wanting a divorce, and the amount for a lawyer. The entire world was against me. I'd never done anything before to cause my family pain. My dumbfounded parents called Grandpa.

It was midnight when the knock came. Grandpa was quickly at my side, reassuring me I'd make it through this. His face was full of pain, and concern was etched in every line of his withered face. I'd never seen fear in his eyes. It was the same fear that pulsed through every vein in my body.

Grandpa wanted me to get away for a while. After a week, he came to visit in Vegas. We walked the Strip together. It was a hot day, so we stopped for a slushy, headed to Circus Circus to watch the trapeze artist, and hit the buffet. Then we went to church together— just him and me, like the good ol' days.

As we walked, he said he soon wouldn't be walking this much. I brushed it off, for he was the healthiest man I knew. Back at Ron's, he tipped me $20 when I made him breakfast. When it was time for him to leave, he told me to stop watching scary movies.

I didn't see him again until I got back from the Dells. Like Monopoly, the warrant was issued, and I went straight to jail. I'll forever picture him standing by his work van the day I turned myself in. He waved at me in his black cap and green work pants. I can't imagine how he felt watching his oldest grandchild walk into jail, like a lamb to the slaughter.

Grandpa waited outside with a few thousand dollars. It was the supposed amount for my bond. Unfortunately, the judge wasn't gracious and set it higher. To my lawyer's surprise, Grandpa replied, "I've banked here for forty years. I'll get a loan. She's my granddaughter. There's nothing I wouldn't do for her." I was bonded out the quickest they'd seen.

The moment I stepped out of jail, Grandpa and Grandma took us out to eat. That's what they did. After church, we went for lunch. Whenever life got tough, you could count on a good meal.

When life got tough ...

Mike and I moved into Grandpa's basement because the local news crews wouldn't stop driving by my house. I helped him all summer on house projects. He said he was getting old and wouldn't be around much longer. I just laughed. He always hopped everywhere he went. Grandpa longed for homemade meals, so I got cracking. He ate like a king. The chicken parmesan was the grand finale.

That night we heard a thud, then Grandma screamed. We rushed to find Grandpa on the floor. He sat up but refused an ambulance because he was a retired firefighter and didn't want the guys to see him that way. He had to get dressed first—because that was super logical.

We were at the hospital all night until they sent us home the next morning. A few hours later, we were called. He was life-flighted, and I needed to get Grandma there. When we arrived, he was taking off the oxygen mask. He said there was just gas on his chest and not to worry. The doctor said he was having another heart attack, and they wheeled him into surgery.

Grandma and I were in the waiting room when we heard a code blue. I just knew it was him. They couldn't get the stent in because he was too weak from the strokes. He was unresponsive and on a breathing machine.

The doctors encouraged us to talk to him. I read him his favorite, Psalm 23. I played Elvis every day and held his hand. I roamed the halls to stay sane but wouldn't leave. I slept in the waiting room outside his room. The nurses said they'd never seen a more devoted granddaughter. Doctors said he was unresponsive, paralyzed, and they'll take the tube out.

A piece of my heart died with him. His wake was on Independence Day, with the funeral the next. We drove past the fire station with all the trucks pulled out and firefighters standing at attention. Grandpa was a vet, so they shot off guns at his gravesite. I jumped at every bullet as the sound felt like nails in a coffin. I'm thankful I was with him in his final days and hold it as a precious gift. I'm thankful he didn't watch me get cuffed away that day. It would've broken his heart.

October 24, 2007

Christiana is my TA friend. She asked me to play on her team for the volleyball tournament. It's more like she told me. Then she read a pamphlet out loud, "You may not be famous, but you matter." Then she said, "Yeah, right, I'm not famous. I was on America's Most Wanted." I thought it was bad that "Inside Edition" wanted to write a report on me. It's crazy, thinking women here have been on the news as well.

I was promoted to Mrs. R's assistant as lead TA. She and I talked over break, and I got to know her better. She homeschooled her children using the same curriculum that comes from our college and had visited our church before. She said God has a plan for us working together. I wish our days weren't so hectic. I'd love to be able to talk like this more often. We end up on opposite sides of the room. I feel like I live with a saint by day and the devil of prison by night.

After supper, I walked while memorizing verses. A couple of women came and shared their stories. I encouraged them with the Scripture I've been learning. They kept asking questions, and the Scripture kept flowing out of me like a water fountain. Before long, we had walked for hours. It was so exciting that I wasn't even phased by the multiple pat searches we received.

October 25, 2007

I was finally able to call you! I'm extremely thankful to start my day by talking with you. I took talking to you for granted. Not being able to talk to or see you for three weeks made me realize it.

The Department of Education is pulling Metro college classes from all institutions. Several inmates are upset, including the one located in the bunk below me. Filth and excessive cursing are currently pouring from her mouth. Unfortunately, her behavior isn't unique to this situation. She often slams doors and throws things, including herself, all over the room. She's constantly cutting others down. It drives me nuts. I would've been able to take college classes, but now that's out for me too.

The judge said I'd receive many programs I could only get in prison. I only have one program and have to wait to be interviewed. The probation office had way more programs. Why wasn't that good enough?

It's weird watching women on the news charged with heavy crimes, knowing they're headed here. I don't watch the news often, but my bunkmate watches relentlessly. She takes it upon herself to tell me everything with a venomously judging tongue. I'd hate to be judged by her. She still doesn't know why I'm here. Anyway, I'd rather not know what other murderers are coming in.

October 26, 2007

My mom and grandma are coming tonight! I haven't seen Grandma since I left the courtroom. I'm sure it'll be difficult for her to see me in prison. I get that you have to work Fridays and can't visit. I'm thankful you'll be able to come on Saturdays and Sundays. Plus, it'll give others the opportunity to see me when you can't.

School is always busy. Most TAs grade while I pop around teaching in both rooms. If students don't pass their tests, they're put into a more difficult book. Some books far exceed anything they'll be tested on. Most TAs struggle with homework and steer clear of helping students. The students get angry at the TAs if they don't understand. The students all come to me, as I'm able to teach them.

We received our Hickory Farms order form. Women get seriously excited about this. It's the only thing our families can purchase for us for Christmas. The excitement is catching. I'll include what I'd enjoy on the back page, but anything is fine.

I received my shoe order form back, but a guard forgot to sign it. It'll take months to get my shoes in. Anything is more comfortable than these boots, but I'll continue walking in them. It's my out. Well, it's almost time to see my mom and grandma.

I absolutely hate being strip-searched before and after visiting. I do it because I desperately want to see those I love. Grandma's extremely sad I'm here. She went from having Grandpa and us to being alone. She's bitter that I got so much time. I agree, but getting worked up kills me. I tried to stay positive and upbeat.

My mother was distant, discouraged, and quiet. It was difficult to watch them cry as they left. I rocked my brave face until they were gone. When they rounded the corner out of sight, my tears came. I can't imagine watching your daughter stay behind locked doors.

October 27, 2007

I finally get to see you after three long weeks, and I can't wait! I feel like I'm floating on air, but I need to stop staring at the clock. The days fly when I'm hustling at school, but weekends drag on. I get to see you today and tomorrow. I'm all giddy. I can feel surges of joy rush through my veins. I have to go walk this out.

I just got back from seeing you. Why does our short visit have to fly? Oh, that my sentence would go that fast. It wasn't too difficult leaving because I know you'll be back tomorrow. You looked so incredibly handsome. I feel like I'm attracted to you more each time I see you. I truly love you like no other. Goodnight.

October 28, 2007

Nicole woke up "off the chain." Apparently, a certain group of women in our hall are too loud. She started a storm of cursing hailstones about how ungrateful they are. She slammed everything she could get her hands on, turned on every light, and cranked up her TV. If she wasn't sleeping, we weren't going to either.

Nicole's sensitive if we make noise when she's trying to sleep. If my blanket, foot, or even a toe hangs off my bed, she freaks. I can't wait until count is cleared and I can get out of this cell. I'm looking forward to seeing you and going to church.

I just got back from seeing you. Thank you for listening to me complain. I love looking into your gorgeous face and baby-blue eyes. Your eyes captivate and whisk me far away from here. I hate watching you leave.

I have more drama. Daisy was afraid to go into our cell because Nicole threatened to strangle her in her sleep. I've not seen Daisy so scared. I told Daisy I'll be with her, and Nicole's just being crazy. Daisy was paranoid and talked to a guard who can't do anything. Daisy's only option is to put herself into PC [Protective Custody].

Daisy finally consented to go into our cell. We did a Bible study very quietly. It went well, and she shared things she needed to get right. Afterward, Nicole said with a large grin on her face, "I'm so glad we have a happy cell!" I think she seriously may be crazy, but at least Daisy felt more comfortable.

October 29, 2007

After dinner, I walked until Bible study. Pat, a woman from school, pointed at me and told her friend that I was her favorite TA. I soaked that in as I fixed my eyes on the amazing sunset unfolding before me. The orange and pink swirled for a beautiful display over the cornfield. It took my breath away, and for a moment, I felt like I'd fly away from this place. Oh, there's no place like home. The sunsets here are incredible, or maybe I've finally slowed down enough to watch them. God brilliantly displayed His light on the dark canvas of prison. Others were also caught up in the beauty, and I exclaimed, "Who can say there's not a God after witnessing something so incredibly breathtaking?"

Monday night Bible study was fantastic. A few older farmers from a nearby church came and shared God's word. They shower love in ways that feel like God Himself. Al and Nadine Peters are an amazing couple who faithfully come each Monday. They gave me a hug that felt so warm and sincere. I instantly loved them. We also sang! I was able to pick a song from their list. I knew most songs and chose "As the Deer."[2] I'm sure I sang much too loudly, but my soul longed to sing. The last song was "Open the Eyes of My Heart,"[3] and I couldn't stop the tears falling from my eyes.

Mail just came, and I received several letters. Your mom said she wrote Daisy and sent her money. I thought Daisy would've received her letter, but she didn't. Daisy could've used that tonight. She's really depressed. She's sobbing and said she hates her life.

I can't believe it! The guard just returned with a letter for her! Apparently, he found another letter. I silently prayed it was from your mom, and she feels the love of Christ awaken her. I got up to use the restroom and saw the letter was from Cheryl. Daisy didn't say anything, but I pray it gets ahold of her heart.

It's amazing how many people back home open up about their deep struggles. I'm thankful I have time to pray and write them. God's at work through my time in prison.

October 30, 2007

Daisy talked to Terry about her problems with Nicole. Daisy didn't know that Terry and Nicole are friends and used to be roommates.

---

[2] "As The Deer," (Maranatha Praise Inc.; Martin Nystrom), 1984.
[3] "Open the Eyes of My Heart," *Open the Eyes of My Heart*, (Integrity Music; Paul Baloche), 2000.

Terry told Nicole everything Daisy said. Nicole went off the rails, and somehow I got roped in. Nicole proceeded to attack me with all the rumors she's heard about me. Nicole scared Daisy into the corner while I stood strong and tried to resolve the issue. God's in control and has not given me the spirit of fear. I don't want to appear weak or an easy target, but I feel a storm brewing.

CHAPTER 5

Rumors

Nicole's watching the news coverage about the teacher on the run with her underaged student. Nicole venomously said if anyone touched her fifteen-year-old, she'd kill them. I keep a quiet distance and pray. She feels like an enemy right now. I'm trying not to think about how she's here for murder.

I'm trying to read my Bible, but I can't concentrate with her TV on at full volume. Nicole continues to rant and adds she's heard rumors about me. She doesn't go into what she's heard, but she's making the connection more and more. She continues to spew out more threats of what she'd do if her baby son would endure something like that.

My stomach is in knots, and I can't sleep. Psalm 22:11 says, "Be not far from me; for trouble is near; and there is none to help." Psalm 23:4, "Yea, though I walk through the valley of the shadow of death, I will fear no evil [that is brewing under my bed]; thy rod and thy staff, they comfort me."

Where's my comfort tonight? Comfort is sleeping in your arms in my own bed. I don't know how long I'll be locked up. I want to go home. Why would God put me in a cell with such a vicious person? Haven't I faced my past and shame long enough?

What lurks under me? I feel something else in this cell. "God has not given you the spirit of fear, but of power, and of love, and of a sound mind" (2 Timothy 1:7). I can't get down like this. Psalm 27:1 says, "The Lord is my light and my salvation, whom shall I fear? The Lord is the strength of my life; of whom shall I be afraid?" When God is my strength, I'm not afraid of anyone.

Nicole's spreading awful things about Daisy. Daisy wants to PC herself in Segregation for three days so she can get a different cell. I asked her, what happens if she gets a worse cellmate when she gets out? I know God put me in this room for a reason.

October 31, 2007

Halloween is all tricks and no treats. I told Nicole that I know there's rumors flying about me. The papers weren't truthful, and I don't appreciate anyone judging me, as I try not to judge others. She seemed to accept my answer. She said Terry told her I didn't say anything about her, only Daisy. I felt the tension lift a bit.

I went for a walk, and a woman joined me. She shared that her young nephew was hit and killed by a car. She asked why God would let that happen to a child. She doubted He'd protect her while she's here. I looked up and prayed. I said that we live in a broken world that wasn't God's plan. This precious child passing wasn't what God intended, and He grieves as we do. He promises to use this for good. This child's now in Heaven with his Creator, who can love him beyond what any human can. He's no longer bound by this world and isn't suffering. He's in the arms of an Almighty God, secured forever.

The words flowed and must've been the answer she needed. She replied, "You're absolutely correct. I never thought of it like that. You were sent to prison just to talk with me." I encouraged her to trust God for protection and was also preaching to myself.

November 1, 2007

Would you send me a calendar? In fact, both my cellmates want one. It'd be nice if Nicole received something. Daisy loves Care Bears and wanted me to throw that out there. Imagine, a woman in prison loving Care Bears. I'd love a tropical one with blank boxes so I can make a fat checkmark on each passing day.

I was talking with a TA in the Commons when Sasha walked up. She saw me on the news and asked what grade I taught on the outs. Sasha said, "I can't believe you'd do something like that. It's such a shame. You're just so pretty." I tried not to say anything, but the silence was awkward. I only said not to believe everything you hear. The TA piped up, "Brandy's a very nice girl, and I don't care."

When Sasha walked away, my friend told me not to cry. I didn't, but I'm upset. Why do they have to rehash it? Each day, someone new learns and stirs it up all over again. Every day, the door opens, revealing the skeleton of my past. It's easier to move on when it's not publicized daily on TV. I'm cracked wide open for all to see.

I felt paranoid the rest of the day. Several women glared and pointed at me. I feel rejected, despised, ashamed, and embarrassed all over again. I picture myself on an unstable boat. In the distance, I see Jesus. I want to get to Him, but I'll have to walk on water. Shackled to my ankles are lead weights of my past. I'm sinking and cannot rise above the chasm of darkness. All I ever do is cry out.

November 3, 2007

Psalm 69:19, "Blessed be the LORD, who daily loath us with benefits." I don't remember this verse, but I sure like it. Even in prison, I receive His blessings. My favorite is seeing you tonight!

Another great visit! I'm swept away from here for a time, and I'm your wife again. I hear about your world so vastly different from mine. I intently watch your face, trying to memorize your features, because I forget that first after you leave. I try to record the sound of your voice, so I can replay it later when I'm trying to fall asleep. I wish I could follow you out the gate to freedom. Instead, I get stripped down before walking through the razor-wire fence that leads back to my literal prison.

I couldn't sleep, so I read. Psalm 78:70, "He chose David also his servant, and took him from the sheepfolds." God knew David would fail on a massive level. David would've been locked up for murder. Out of all the men God could choose, God chose David because of his heart. People often judge on the outside, but God chooses what man cannot see.

Psalm 86:14–17, "O God, the proud are risen against me, and assemblies of violent men have sought after to kill me..." The proud people remind me of Christians who've rejected me. When God talks about the violent man, I think of women here. These women plague me with questions, looks, and judging eyes.

I'm called to love both groups and am certainly not above anyone. To be honest, I'd rather be sought after by prisoners than judgmental Christians. I'm glad this verse continues, "But thou, O LORD, art a God full of compassion, gracious, long suffering, and plenteous in mercy and truth. O turn unto me, and have mercy upon me, give thy strength unto thy servant, and save the son of thine handmaid. Show me a token for good; that they which hate me may see it, and be ashamed because thou, LORD, hast helped me, and comforted me."

I need to pray for everyone that rises against me. We're called to love first and foremost. God's forgiveness isn't limited, and I desire it for all. People from church hurt me to the core of my being. They not only rejected me, but my family as well. It's not right to accept some sinners and withhold love from others. I didn't recognize it at the time, but I looked to the church to define who God was. God is now revealing Himself to me.

Church was amazing! The speakers, Steve and Diane Collins, did prison time and currently run a halfway house. Steve spoke from places others can't simply because they haven't experienced prison or understand what I'm going through. I often feel like I had great gifts, but ruined my opportunity to do great things for God. I had great potential, but I blew it. Hearing how God is using them gives me hope He can use me as well. Hope is so powerful. I want God to use me to restore hope to the hopeless.

November 5, 2007

I went to Monday Bible study. Unfortunately, two women were whispering about how horrible I am the whole time. I tried to ignore them and focus on the lesson. But, seriously, in church?

Your mom sent me a beautiful Bible. I absolutely love it! I can't wait to write on all the pages. Your grandmother wrote me and titled it, "My favorite granddaughter," and sent, "Big bear hugs and kisses." Your family is such a blessing. They seriously sustain me. I've got a Bible study that I'll teach in our lobby.

My JCPenny order form was returned due to the small blue designs on my long johns being "Gang-related." I doubt I'll ever receive anything.

November 6, 2007

I was called into Medical for another shot. The nurse said she had to get my DNA because of my charge. I thought it was weird, but it's not like I have options. She asked about my offense in front of all the nursing students in the room. I said, "Attempted sexual assault." She then asked for my release date, and I said, "2011."

Then this nurse announces to everyone that I'm lying. She said I received too much time for attempted, so my charge must be straight-up sexual assault. I explained there was a discussion about this when I first went into Segregation, so my caseworker called the courthouse and reviewed everything, and it's indeed "attempted." I just received a greater sentence than almost every attempted sexual assault case. The nurse tried to argue with me. I stopped talking and allowed her to stab my arm and take my blood. The added bonus was a room full of gawking people who assumed the worst about me.

I went straight back to work and struggled all day. I felt like a leaky bucket and fought back tears. I'm attacked every single day. I'm so tired. When will this all end?

"Forever," is the word I heard screamed at me. I'll live with this forever. I want to crawl into a hole and never come out. I'll have to register for years with this label branded on my life. Brandy's sin, exposed for all to judge. The words "It hurts" cannot express what I'm feeling inside. I kited my caseworker explaining what happened. That I can do. What I can't do is get over this constant feeling of humiliation.

I fear this is something I'll face daily as long as I breathe. I'm considered "violent." It breaks my heart that the law attaches this horrendous label to my life for all to see. I know there's nothing I can do, and ultimately, God is in control. I just really hurt. I want a freaking hug, just one stinking hug, a good ol' bear hug. A physical touch of reassurance that even though this epically sucks, everything will be okay.

Pain and more pain. I cannot wait until I'm in Heaven and there's no more pain.

November 7, 2007

I'm glad I started my day by talking with you. Christina (the one who was on America's Most Wanted) was also in the Marines. A student told Christina that she didn't want me helping her because I'm a child molester. Thankfully, Christina stuck up for me.

At lunch, I overheard a table talking about me. When I looked up, they all stared at me. A new batch of inmates was released, and I'm the talk of the yard all over again. I'm ready to throw in the towel and go home. *Oh wait,* I can't go home.

Christina says they attack me because I'm smart, pretty, nice, have support, letters, visits, and friends. These women are jealous and want to tear me down. I don't want to come off better than anyone. I know I've been given more than most here, and I don't take that for granted. I suppose tearing others down gives them something to think about other than the junk going on inside themselves.

I try to keep my head up, but it's a never-ending battle. It's a deep wound that starts healing, and then someone rips off the bandaid. I'll have to face these attacks for the rest of my life.

My sister sent me a picture of her trying on wedding dresses. I cried, thinking about all that I'm missing. The catalog people lost my order, so now I have no idea when I'll get my stuff. I'm depressed. It's time to read my Bible.

November 9, 2007

I just found out that my screening for LRC is Tuesday morning. I finally know the day. This determines where I'll go, how long I'll stay, and what happens to me. Just when my poor heart finally settles down, it's back up to an uncontrollable gallop like a wild horse that doesn't know where to run.

Sasha's spreading vicious rumors about me. I pray God shuts the mouths of these lions. Their glares and words haunt me. I know I need to respond with love, but a caterpillar doesn't turn into a butterfly in only three weeks. I feel I'm in the vicious cycle of tearing, bleeding, and healing in the cocoon of prison. I suppose it's part of the process of change. I need to develop a tough skin. How else will I make it through life with people constantly judging me based on my label? I'll have to learn now.

A thought flashed into my mind: "Is living a life like this worth it?" I feel subhuman. I'll always be the one who has to earn her place in society. My heart fails to rise in the deep pain. My lungs wither, and it's difficult to breathe. I know my life isn't my own, but this wasn't what I had planned. This isn't who I'd dreamed of being.

I told Daisy about my appointment Tuesday and she bawled. She was crying so hard that she couldn't speak. She said she couldn't handle prison without me. I don't want to leave either, despite all the evil and rumors. I don't want to go to a mental hospital and start all over. I'm trying to come forth as gold, but the fire is very hot.

As 2 Corinthians 4:8–9 says, "We are troubled on every side, yet not distressed, we are perplexed, but not in despair; Persecuted, but not forsaken, cast down, but not destroyed." My focus must be on the eyes of Jesus and not on the waters upon waters of destruction surrounding me. When will I be able to finally trust? I feel so helpless to the roaring emotions brewing inside me.

Nicole said we can't talk in our cell, so we headed to the noisy lobby. We had several women ask to join our study. Keep praying for Nicole. I think she's having a little breakthrough. She said I've inspired her to start reading her Bible. She called me "normal," and said that she appreciates me. I about fell off of my bunk.

November 12, 2007

I've met others attacked by vindictive lies and assaulting tongues. Several inmates prey on women, verbally assaulting and threatening them in hopes they'll PC themselves. I'm thankful God has put a few friends in here that defend against these attacks, but unfortunately, most aren't in my housing unit.

God often breathes a melody when fear surrounds me. Psalm 143:8, "Cause me to hear thy lovingkindness in the morning; for in thee do I trust; cause me to know the way wherein I should walk, for

I lift up my soul unto thee." Psalm 138:7–8, "Though I walk in the midst of trouble, thou wilt revive me: thou shalt stretch forth thine hand against the wrath of mine enemies, and thy right hand shall save me. The LORD will perfect that which concerneth me."

The Wizard of Oz was on. I silently joked to myself, thinking, "It'd be easier if a house would drop on the wicked witches of the North Hall." I liked Glinda's advice, "It's best to start at the beginning. All you have to do is follow [God's] yellow brick road." I need to keep putting one foot in front of the other. Truly, there's no place like home.

It helped, watching my favorite movie, so I wasn't focusing on the meeting tomorrow with LRC. I've covered it with prayer, but now I'm nervous. Lord, help me sleep and get me through tomorrow.

CHAPTER 6

The Interview

November 13, 2007

The meeting was delayed by forty minutes. Two older women dressed in suits arrived and led me to a private room. The first few questions were basic background information. Then they asked how the relationship developed.

I started by saying I was the adult and responsible for all that happened. I began telling the story, with them asking questions throughout. Their perspective for the entire relationship was focused on the first time. When I explained how the first time had happened, their whole demeanor changed. They said somehow I'd forced him to do that to me. Everything he did or said, I was completely responsible for. He was not his own person. It was as if he were an infant and not a teenager.

Their reply was the same from then on: "You are lying to yourself." They shut the door of communication. They didn't believe anything I said. They asked when I last talked to him. I said it's been over a year. They didn't believe me. They assured me I'd been fantasizing about him, which I haven't. I prayed God would remove any thoughts from the past. I'm extremely exhausted and disgusted.

I'm repulsed by going to that awful place. I'll have to deal with this questioning every day for two years. How can this brainwashing garbage benefit me? I don't want to think about those things they're suggesting. I don't think like that. I don't know if they're trying to get me to break or what they're attempting to accomplish. I think it went horribly, and all I can do is cover it with prayer.

I'm so tired of all these questions, disgusting tests, and lies. God doesn't give me more than I can handle? I can't handle this! I want to go home. I'm so tired. I'm at the bottom of the ocean and feel the weight of the water flowing over my body. I'm drowning. I'm obeying, praying, and giving everything I have. So why this? I tried calling you, but you didn't answer.

What's on TV nonstop? The teacher who kidnapped her student and took him across borders. My mind is rehashing that horrible interview. The doctor constantly interrupted me, "How is that? We know you forced him." It plays on repeat, and I feel like I'm going to puke again. There's nothing I can do. I have to put this fear and dread out of my mind for two months. I think that's how long they said before I'd hear back.

I feel completely drained and have to go back to work. I need to talk to you. Today was one of the worst days of my entire life. I can't eat. I know I can't lose hope, but mine is hanging on by a thread.

All day I've heard bits and pieces of what it's like there: brainwashing classes all day. You can't have a job because you're in full-time programming. They treat you like nothing. If it were like I was treated today, I believe it. If I deny programming, I'll be here for four years or more. That's not an option, but I feel like I'll lose my mind there. Every fiber of my being is screaming at me. If they reject me, then I do four years here because I don't qualify. There's only one person I've heard that completed the program. The men have this program in their prison, so why can't we have one here? I'm starting to have problems breathing.

I couldn't stop crying, so I went to see my caseworker. All she knew was a few have gone and never came back. The caseworkers look at me with blank faces. All of their training didn't prepare them for this. They aren't prepared for me. I've been trying not to let anyone see me. Tears have rolled down my face all day. I feel like I was hit by a truck. I'm physically, emotionally, spiritually, and mentally drained. I see no way out. Can you find out if I lose two years for good behavior if I reject the program? I'm sure my lawyer is busy with his new teacher case.

Everyone asks what's wrong. I thought about calling my parents, but I'll just worry and stress them. Psalm 69:18–20, "Draw nigh unto my soul, and redeem it: deliver me because of mine enemies. Thou hast known my reproach, and my shame, and my dishonor, mine adversaries are before thee. Reproach hath broken my heart; and I am full of heaviness; I looked for some to take pity, but there was none, and for comforters, but I found none." I will be up as early as my door opens to call you.

November 15, 2007

I've struggled with every breath. I was finally doing something fun by coloring a turkey picture with Daisy in the hall. Once again, I'm approached by someone I don't know saying, "I've been just dying to ask you how many years you got?"

I'm attacked by fear, depression, homesickness, judgments, or when something bad happens. It's a stab in the back that sends me facedown back into the pit. I want to leave it at the feet of Jesus. He won't let anything bad happen to me, even mentally, right? In the pit of my stomach, I believe I'm going there.

God sometimes chooses not to deliver us, right? I'm in prison now. With God, I can handle being a prisoner physically, but what about mentally? Psalm 91:9–11; 14–16, "Because thou hast made the LORD, which is my refuge, even the most High, thy habitation; there shall no evil befall thee, neither shall any plague come nigh unto thy dwelling. For He shall give his angels charge over thee, to keep thee in all thy ways..."

I know my main problem is fear. I've been giving it over, and then my mind wanders. I'm mentally exhausted. I'll see my caseworker tomorrow, and I'm afraid of what she'll say. See, fear again.

I understand you want to be with your family for Thanksgiving, but it's difficult. I'm dreading the holidays here. I don't think you realize how much I need you. I'm heartsick for you. Can you arrange for my family to come visit me while you're gone? I hate holiday commercials.

Isaiah 41:13, "For I the Lord thy God will hold thy right hand, saying unto thee, Fear not, I will help thee." Proverbs 1:33, "But whoso hearkeneth unto me shall dwell safely, and shall be quiet from fear of evil." Isaiah 14:3, "The Lord shall give thee rest from thy sorrow, and from thy fear, and from the hard bondage wherein thou wast made to serve." I'm in the thick of the hard bondage.

I finally received my JCPenny order back. It didn't apply the free shipping. Shipping is $18, which is two weeks of work. Can't anyone do their job? I wish I could do things myself. I absolutely hate having to depend on others to do my laundry, cook my food, go through my mail, and complete my forms incorrectly. I'll pay the extra money. I can't wait another week to send this in. My feet are in so much pain.

November 16, 2007

I hope my dad comes to visit tonight. It's difficult to think of going another two months without seeing him if I have to leave. There's nothing I can do except pray for the best, but I've come to expect the worst.

I received no visit tonight. I probably looked pretty pathetic sitting in my outfit, waiting for my name to be called for two hours. A proper ending for the week I've had. I just watched *Titanic,* making me miss you even more. As I pen these words, the couple drowns in the middle of the freezing Atlantic Ocean.

November 17, 2007

God's mercies are new every morning, and I'm so grateful that I awoke to a beautiful day. I was thankful for the warmth and took my Bible outside. I needed the sun on my face as it awoke the Son in my heart to speak to me.

Soon after I prayed, I looked around and was no longer alone. Many women came to join, bearing their hearts and struggles. Together we clung to the living Word and prayed for each other. I happened to have extra Thanksgiving coloring sheets I'd received in the mail, so we all colored for a while and continued our conversations. It was a good day, and we needed it.

I loved the letter you sent and will keep it in my Bible. You said you can't live without me, your heart belongs to me alone, and you're not going anywhere. I feel the pain you're experiencing as well. Never make light of what you're going through because of where I'm at.

I'm sorry I cried and clung onto you at Visiting tonight. I didn't want to let go. I don't want to be here. I don't want to be strip-searched, violated, and walked back through the metal doors. I want to go home and leave this awful place.

November 18, 2007

The music awards are on. "I'm going home to the place that I belong, where your love has always been enough for me. I'm running home; faith has got me on the road. I don't regret the life you chose for me.

These places and these faces are getting old. So I'm going home."[4] Amen, Daughtry.

You looked gorgeous today in your regular clothing. It's so nice to see normal clothes. I see khaki everywhere. I dream of people wearing khaki. I wish I had a camera and could capture the moment I got lost in your blue eyes. I'd stare into your calm face forever.

Your encouragement is fuel for my empty shell. I prayed you'd have words to comfort my raging heart. You're my human hero. Your visits, calls, letters, and everything you do keeps me going. I'm proud to be your wife. I'll miss you greatly this Thanksgiving. I'm very thankful for you. You're the one who carries my torch.

My heart melted when you called me "strong." We both know I have no strength. Anything I have comes from God. I'm glad you are proud of me. I was afraid you would be ashamed of my struggles. You grow nearer to my heart each time I see you. I couldn't do this without your love, support, prayers, and encouragement.

I received several letters tonight. The first I read was from my sister's friend. She said I'm the godly example she looks up to. She's encouraged by how I'm handling what I'm going through. Both my sisters and your sisters not only all wrote me at the same time, but also wrote the same thing. My heart cries, "What? No young women should be looking up to me! I'm in prison." It makes me want to be strong because these girls/women look up to me, and I certainly don't want to fall again.

My sister sent me pictures of when we were children. Knowing the smiling, brown-headed girl is currently sitting in prison is difficult. I would never have believed I'd be here. I can't wait to see you when you come up on Sunday.

---

[4] "Home," *Duaghtry*, (RCA 19 Warner; Daughtry), 2007.

November 20, 2007

School was hectic. It's a challenge jumping to each student because I can go from a 2nd-grade level to an 11th-grade level. The curriculum is horrible. Math and language are the worst because you need to build on a solid foundation. Most of these women don't have a foundation at all, which is probably the story of their lives. The students get frustrated and want answers immediately, but I have to read the directions and figure out what's expected. By that time, the student is mad.

November 21, 2007

I accidentally put my khakis in the wrong bin this morning. I had to dig through everyone's dirty underwear to find my bag; otherwise, I get written up. Women glared at me while making stupid comments about the sex offender going through dirty laundry.

My cellmate is in a bad mood and doesn't want to watch the Thanksgiving parade. Thankful things I miss most are you, my family, friends, puppies, Christmas shopping at the mall, Auntie Anne's pretzels, ice cream, Texas Roadhouse, going to a movie, sunbathing, walking, biking, road trips, listening to music, working in our yard, cooking, decorating cakes, Starbucks, renting a movie, baths, clothes, contacts, the smell of clean laundry, my purse, wedding ring, church, fuzzy socks, furry coats, my soft bed, blankets, and fluffy pillows. I could go on, but I'm depressed now.

November 23, 2007

Last night, Nicole was off the chain. As she shook our bed, Daisy started having meth cravings. She's seven months sober. She said she'd relapse if she wasn't in prison. At this point, Nicole finally fell asleep.

I told Daisy to breathe deeply and wash her face and hands. Then she started shaking. Something popped into my mind, so I went with it. I cranked out the bag of gummy bears I'd been saving and told her this would do the trick. She's having meth cravings, and I offered her gummy bears! We gut-wrenching laughed for a good five minutes. After the bears, she cracked open her Bible to Psalms and finally fell asleep. I made it through another day in prison. Check.

November 24, 2007

Bible study was frustrating. I need an easier study for these women. They need basics with more interaction and less reading. Also, the noise is unbearable. I'm literally yelling the verses when we read. There are many interruptions with women constantly coming and going.

More drama stirs around the holidays. Women are off work, everyone misses their family, and there's nothing to do. Nicole's still upset and now Daisy's upset about something. I'm going outside.

I wish we had revivals in prison. I want to go to church every day. It seems like I kinda dreaded revivals when they came to church or college. I feel terrible for saying that, and it's only because they took so much time out of my busy schedule. I just went through the motions. All I want to do here is go to church.

I enjoyed the church service on TV more than the one that came in today. I ended up leaving since what they taught wasn't biblical. Any "church" can come and teach whatever they want. Psalm 29:11 says, "The Lord will give strength unto his people; the Lord will bless his people with peace." Peace amidst the storm, that's what I need— to settle into peace.

November 29, 2007

I'm SO HAPPY! I got my CD player and the Casting Crowns CD today. I haven't heard any Christian music for two months. I'm so thankful for music! I feel my soul take flight as if I can escape for a little while. I'm on my bunk listening to "Praise You in This Storm"[5] as Nicole is swearing at the top of her lungs while shaking my bed.

"Though my heart is torn, I'll praise You in this storm. I lift my eyes unto the hill; where does my help come from? My help comes from the Lord." I lift my eyes to the window and see the razor wire. I thought God would've saved my day by now, but I will praise God in this storm.

Music has brought a pep to my step. I smiled and greeted everyone on my way to school. It reminds me of the fifteen-foot rule when I worked at Walmart. If someone looked lost, we'd ask, "Is there anything I can help you with?" Isn't it the same with us? When someone appears lost in the great store of life, shouldn't we ask, "Is there any way I can help?"

Pat's the older lady from school that I help. She told me today that she has AIDS. Pat's a fighter who doesn't care what others think, which inspires me. She always defends me by saying that she has a fifteen-year-old son and she'd trust me with her life.

Later, as I waited for a seminar called "New You," a group of students walked by. Pat pointed at me and said in front of everyone, "Brandy, you don't need a new you; you're perfect the way you are." I was a little embarrassed, but it spoke volumes to my heart.

Several TAs get out of prison soon. I'll get one of their pay spots of $3.78 a day. That's the most I can make in prison, so I'm grateful. Mrs. R also said I'm doing an amazing job, and she's extremely grateful for me.

---

[5] "Praise You in This Storm," *Lifesong,* (Beach Street and Reunion Records; Casting Crowns), 2006.

I didn't have to listen to my cellmates complain when I got to my cell. I just slipped on my headphones. Listening to music rather than their bickering is surreal. I feel like I'm in my own little bubble.

Mary's my closest walking friend. She sweetly associates herself with me and thus has associated herself with Jesus. She had a visit with her three-year-old today. Mary hasn't seen him for three months and was afraid he'd forgotten her. After her visit, she found me with tears streaming down her face. Her son wouldn't let her go when it was time to leave. His caseworker had to pull him away from her.

My heart broke, but I reminded her, "This is what we prayed for. We prayed he'd be able to visit, that he'd remember you, and want to be with you."

She smiled through the tears and said that she wanted me to leave with her next month. I told her I wished that too, but that God goes with her. He's a closer friend than I could ever be. I pray she continues to go to Him for all her answers.

December 3, 2007

Terry needed help today. She was desperate, swallowed her pride, and asked me. She's never asked me before. I silently prayed as I walked to her. She's pretty close to being done with her GED. She's in higher math, but I broke it down for her. She understood and got all her problems right.

Now she writes my name on the board next to hers for help. I just stared at our names next to each other. I can't explain it. She had spread lies and hated me. It all vanished when she said, "I only understand when you explain it." I hope one day I can share more than math. I want to break down walls Satan puts up. Hopefully, when women get to know me, it silences the gossip, rumors, and hate.

Daisy plugged her headphones into my player and listened to Christian music with me. She took her headphones off and looked up at me from her bunk. I took off my headphones as she fought back tears. She said, "One day, I'm going to get through these years in prison. I'll grow in God and learn. I'll tell my story. If you hear your name, it's because you got me this far." I told her it wasn't me that got her this far; it was God. I'm blessed He used me to help her.

December 7, 2007

My dad came to visit me tonight. I hadn't seen him in two months. The visit was difficult at first. We've never really talked a lot. Two hours without distractions was a challenge. Toward the end, he asked about the LRC and said he's worried. Hearing his fears and questions made me scared, and I started crying. I know it tears him up to see me cry, so I tried my best to slap on a smile and change the subject.

December 8, 2007

Snow days are no fun in prison. I dressed for my visit with my mom, but it was canceled. I was the only nut walking outside. The guard pulled me aside and asked what I was reading. I showed him my verse cards. He looked through them and asked why I was doing it. I told him I hide God's Word in my heart, so when I'm afraid or sad, I know what God has to say.

He quizzed me on Psalm 142:6–7, and I knew it. "Attend unto my cry for I am brought very low; deliver me from my persecutors, for they are stronger than I. Bring my soul out of prison so I may praise thy name. The righteous shall compass me about, for thou shalt deal bountifully with me." He was impressed and let me go.

CHAPTER 7

Tisn't the Season

Today was GED graduation. One graduate said she wouldn't be graduating if TAs didn't help her. She acknowledged that TAs have no authority and get hassled constantly.

Our teacher shared a story relating to the TAs. "A little boy was walking up and down a shoreline, and there were hundreds of thousands of starfish that had washed up on the shore. He started picking them up one by one, then more at a time, and throwing them back into the ocean. An old man was watching the boy and said, "What are you doing? Do you really think you're going to do anything? Look at all those starfish. Are you crazy?"

The little boy looked up at him and said, "I may not be able to help all the starfish, but for the ones I was able to throw back, I made a difference."

There are many hurting women that want to give up. I can't give up on people, even when they're mean. I guess that's it; I'm making a difference here. If God wants me at that mental hospital, I can only trust I'll make a difference there. I pray I can lay this at His feet and stop worrying. He's in control and has my best interests at heart.

I'm in complete shock. I was putting my red drink on the shelf, and it basically jumped off. It was a nightmare. It looked like the movie *Carrie* at the Prom. It spilled over the entire room, including Nicole's bed, her Bible, and her clothes. The worst was her Bible. I apologized constantly. It took me three hours to clean up. I thought for certain Nicole would've lost it by cussing, screaming, and throwing objects. She wasn't happy, but she didn't scream at me. She said it was an accident, but indeed bigger than any of her children have ever made. I told her I'd buy her a new Bible.

December 11, 2007

Daisy has to move. They're making A and B Halls for murderers or sex offenders only, and C and D for lesser violent crimes. Nicole's complaining, and Daisy's bawling. I'll miss Daisy's face smiling up at me.

Tomorrow I'm leading a new study I came up with. I hope it's quiet and the women are receptive. We're meeting early, so hopefully, that helps.

December 12, 2007

I didn't get much sleep with the anticipation of teaching this study. It went really well, and several showed up. We had a great discussion, and several opened up and shared their stories. I'm thankful God answered, and we ventured into a deep level.

Two TA friends leave tomorrow who have always had my back. It's difficult to hear their excitement about going to Work Release while I have to stay. My workload has increased. I'm now training new TAs, doing student orientation, and assigning curriculum on top of helping all the students. We have a total of 120 students. Mrs. R better pray I stay; otherwise, the TAs will be swamped.

December 14, 2007

At school, I went to help a student who I've never helped before. She's always angry and I've steered clear of her. She said I'd helped her with her work, and it was all wrong. I kindly said, "I don't remember helping you, but I can." She started groaning and thrusting her body with sharp mannerisms. I tried to calm her down, but she got louder.

I found Mrs. R, explained what happened, and Mrs. R pulled her out of class. Meanwhile, I helped students in the other room. Later, I went back into her room. She swore at me and called me a bunch of names. I ignored her and helped others until class was over.

After class, Mrs. R asked if I was scared to go back to my hall. She said I could PC myself. I'm frustrated. Doesn't she know what Segregation is like? I told her I'd be fine and left. Honestly, I'm nervous because this angry woman lives next door and has life for murder.

Nicole said she and Angry Woman were cellmates. Nicole was constantly physically abused by her. They ended up fighting and both going to Segregation. Angry Woman's the one that yells in our hall, which sets Nicole off. It helped me understand Nicole a bit better.

You told me this morning that Jackie had her baby. I knew she was due soon. I've been having bad dreams. I still hurt. It still feels fresh and is now stirred up. I hate that the baby could be yours. You say it'll never be yours, but I hate it. It feels like Jackie has the upper hand. It's like she holds all the keys. I still see her face smiling at me while I was in pain. It feels like I've lost a part of you, and it eats at me. I want to be far from them. If there's a chance this girl is yours, then there's a chance they could come waltzing in.

I'm alone in a cage, and she's out there possibly rocking your child. How's that fair? I'm staring through my barred-up window, hoping for freedom. Reality is my punishment, and it's only just begun. I'm a doormat everyone wipes their crap onto before going into their homes and living their actual lives. I don't get to go in. No one really wants me, anyway. No one cares about the outside mat. The more crap they take off themselves, the better. They move on and live while I remain.

By God's grace, I need to become more than this. I need to release this anger. I'm trying to walk on water to Jesus. Every obstacle is another wave. My footing is shaken by the roaring of these women. There are strong gusts of women exiting prison while I remain. Throw in the jail system's disorganization and guilty until proven innocent. Thick fog sets in, blinding my way. Will I go to a mental institution and lose my mind?

Every nerve's on fire, attacking my core like a disease. The disease is mine, yours, and everyone's sin, and it cuts deep. The baby's a reminder of all that we went through. How do I walk on water and not allow prison to swallow me up? How do I make it to the other side? In Matthew 14:30, Peter shouted, "Save me, LORD!" I find myself shouting, screaming, begging, wailing through blurred vision and a broken heart. What wrecks me is, "Jesus immediately reached out and grabbed him."

There's no waiting, wondering, or dreaded anticipation. Why is it immediately for Peter and wait for me? Why does He allow me to remain on my life preserver in the midst of the storm? I'm sure it's to teach me. Love doesn't come without a cost, right? Jesus's love for us scarred and killed him. I'm waiting for the sun to shine, water to calm, fog to rise, wind to cease, hail to halt, and the burning to subside. "Oh, what a glorious day that will be."

My tears have stopped. It helped me to write. I prayed for them and am now trying to move on with my day. I've much to learn, and my growth is slow. Sometimes I forget in the dark what I saw in the light. I have to relearn lessons. We will make it through this. One day, we'll rise above the hurt and painful past. I must live like it'll be worth it someday, and I'll see the "why" later. It's my motivation to carry on when it gets difficult. One day, I'll be in your arms. I'll have my life back, marred as it will be. Keep holding my hand through this storm, and never, ever let go, no matter what happens. I promise to do the same.

Comfort flowed when I saw my sister. I bawled when I saw her and hugged her tightly. This day was awful. It felt good to be held in her arms and cry. I'm not sure she's been on that end of our relationship. I'm always the stronger older sister, but she was that for me tonight. The visit went too fast, and I was left to my thoughts.

I just got back from my visit with you. You said I'm starting to doubt God with the possibility of going to LRC, and you're right. After you left, I sat on the bench, waiting to be stripped, and prayed. God knows best, and His promises are true no matter how gloomy the outlook. I made that bench my altar and put God back where He belongs. Pray I rely on Him and not worry about this hospital.

The Lord of the Rings is on. Frodo said, "I'm tired; I don't think I can go on." Frodo was blessed to have a friend. "Stories, the good ones, are about going through hard, dark, impossible ways. We have to carry on; the world depends on us. We have to believe there's something worth fighting for and that there's good still left in this world. I'll help you carry this burden."

Thanks for helping me carry this load when I'm so very tired and for reminding me God will carry us through. He's stronger than all human help combined. That's why He kept cutting back Gideon's army. God demonstrated He owns the battle. He's the author and finisher and writes my story. No good story is without trials and darkness.

The movie's over, the lights are out, and I'm still here without you. I keep thinking I'll wake up from this terrible nightmare, but my time hasn't come. I look at pictures of those I love, and my heart bleeds. I try not to cry out loud; otherwise, I get kicked from below. I truly pray for sweet dreams.

December 17, 2007

The gossip monster's being fed. Terry was accused of cheating at school. She's telling everyone that I turned her in. I was the last to know she was cheating. The incident with Angry Woman spread, so I'm labeled as a snitch. I've never been around so much outlandish garbage. One minute there's success with Terry, and the next, there's backstabbing.

I just finished peeling dead skin off my feet. It was so gross, probably a half-inch thick in places. I seriously have chunks of skin gone from my heels. I'm blessed to have good teeth. Daisy got three more cavities, Mary got a tooth pulled, and Nicole got two teeth filled. Almost everyone has missing or silver teeth because the dentist pulls teeth like a madman.

Pray for Sam as she shares the letter I wrote to my family on Christmas. I understand if you aren't in the mood to see my family for Christmas.

Dear Family,

I'd give anything to be sitting at the cabin with you, but God has other plans this Christmas. I won't be celebrating bright lights, good food, family or presents this year. My focus is solely on the birth of Christ. Although food, family and friends are great, Christmas is all about Jesus.

Christmas is the celebration of the birth of God's only Son sent into this world to live and die for our sins. The bad things I did to get here were nailed on our Savior's cross. He died to set me free. Although I'm not physically free, I'm free on the inside. Without Him, I'd be lost and stuck here without hope. That baby changed the world. He changed my life and continues to change it; day by day, and pain by pain. My prayer is you experience that same love and power in your lives.

This season has been difficult. If it weren't for God's amazing grace, I don't know where I'd be. It's easy to allow depression, fear, and doubt to set in and cloud your vision when going through difficulties. This past year has been the most difficult year of my life.

Praise God for the Bible! I'm happy that all of God's promises are true. "I would have fainted, unless I had believed to see the goodness of the Lord in the land of the living. Wait on the Lord, be of good courage, and he shall strengthen your heart" (Psalm 27:13–14). God talks about fear in Isaiah 41:10: "Don't panic. I'm with you. There is no need to fear, for I am your God." As for my future, "I know the plans for you, declares the Lord, plans for good and not a disaster, to give you a future and hope" (Jeremiah 29:11), and Romans 8:28, "And we know that all things work together for good to those that love God."

"All things" means the good and the bad. How will God use my life for good? So far, He's used me to encourage and share His love with hurting women while I'm here. That's why God sent Jesus to die on the cross two thousand years ago. Christmas isn't just the birth of Christ, but also God's love for us. God gives us the gift of salvation through His greatest love, His Son. Will you accept Him into your life? It's the most important present you'll ever unwrap, but you must choose to accept it. I pray you will. I miss you all! Merry Christmas!

December 19, 2007

I got my Hickory Farms order! There were lots of little meats, cheeses, and candies. One little fudge square does so much for me. Thank you! I cried when I took everything out because I thought of your sacrifice, and it made me miss you all the more. I just had sausage, cheese, and crackers for supper. Real food is amazing!

Our mail is horrible, and some letters arrive before others. The principal from my former school wrote to me. I'd written to him weeks ago, expressing my heart and asking for forgiveness for how I hurt him and the school. I didn't expect him to write back. I don't blame him for being upset, but his letter is extremely condemning and judgmental. He said I should ask the church and Todd's family for forgiveness, and I have.

He said I've not taken responsibility for my actions, and I'm acting more like Saul than David. He also said I was basically a waste as I was the best teacher he had and blew it. I don't understand why he feels he's in a position to weigh that out. I don't need his forgiveness, but I don't need his judgment based on false information.

It's the week before Christmas, and I'm in prison. I've done everything I can and what God put in my heart. Why is forgiveness given to some and not others? Why are some allowed to stay in the fold and others rejected? I'm taking the brunt of everything, just like you said. I suppose it's easy since I'm the felon.

December 20, 2007

The SAU [Substance Abuse Unit] Christmas program was today. Only those in school can attend, since SAU is isolated from the rest of the prison. I was thankful for the break. The program was pretty festive and funny. My favorite part was the woman missing her front tooth singing, "All I want for Christmas is my two front teeth." It was like a kids' Christmas program played by adults. It's nice to see some holiday spirit.

We had new students start Monday. One was Lynn, who had just gotten out of Segregation. She used to be in my bunk. She threatened to break Nicole's TV and face in front of everyone and went to Segregation. Lynn asked for my help. I kindly explained what she needed to correct. She started cussing and moving her body in short bursts of anger. I tried to calm her down, but I didn't get a chance. She zoned out into a full-blown temper tantrum. Mrs. R pulled her into the hall. Lynn screamed at everyone that she wouldn't do her work. Guards were called, and Lynn was escorted back to Segregation.

Many women are receiving cards from your mother. She's quite popular and doing a tremendous work. Everyone comments about how they love her. Mail is both powerful and precious. The hardest of hearts can be melted with love. Mail time is my escape from prison.

December 21, 2007

I've been washing my clothes in the sink with shampoo. Our clothes come back dirtier than when we send them. I have some blisters on my hands from wringing out wet clothes.

Grandma and my sister came to visit. They wanted to talk about the principal's letter. I was not trying to add fuel to the fire, since those two were pretty fiery already. My sister's dealing with her own stuff being cut off from church. Please pray for them. I wished them a Merry Christmas when they left, and Grandma said, "I will not say it, because it will not be merry." The guard that stripped me was rude. It's bad enough that I have to bend and spread it every visit, but when someone is mean, it's just awful.

December 22, 2007

During lockdown, Nicole made a spread for Daisy and me. I think Nicole misses Daisy too. The spread can be used in burritos as well. You chop hot sausage and put it into an empty chip bag. Then add crushed hot triplets [BBQ chips], hot California soup, and jalapeño cheese. We put it on the light to warm it. Scoop up with spicy Doritos and enjoy.

Ruby shared her story with me. She said your mother and I have shown real love. We gave without expecting anything in return. Tears welled in her eyes as she spoke. My eyes drifted to her arms. She usually wears long sleeves, but not tonight. Her arms bear marks from trying to commit suicide. I'm grateful for your mom, grandma, and their friends writing to inmates. They're making a difference for these women.

Christmas Eve, 2007

I led a good study for several women on our hall this morning. The only service was mass. Terry sat in the middle of the yard, venomously glaring at me and singing out her disgusting music. I prayed and worshiped while lapping around her. Pat searches flowed in the lobby all night. It's funny how the cops come out more during the holidays, no matter where you are.

Christmas Day, 2007

Merry Christmas from prison. You're my constant and will enter the gateway of chaotic later for me. I'm sincerely grateful. Unfortunately, it is true, Santa does not visit prison. There's no presents, stockings, lights, trees, or nativity. I did receive Nicole's TV at dawn to drown out Angry Woman. Our neighbor stayed up all night caroling, I mean swearing.

I walked in on several make-out sessions when I showered. Nicole watched *The Christmas Story* twice last night and once this morning. My brain is on repeat, "You're going to shoot your eye out, kid." It doesn't feel like Christmas. I gaze at my Christmas cards, reminding me it's indeed Christmas—time to pick up my Bible.

CHAPTER 8

Scary Terry

December 27, 2007

I joined a program, SALSA (Supporters and Leaders Against Sexual Assault), for those who've been sexually abused. I wanted to work on what happened when I was a child. It's positive to the board to complete programs, and there's nothing else on my list. Several friends signed up with me. We talked on a surface level for two hours.

Afterward, the counselor pulled me aside, saying these women went through significant sexual abuse and may see me as their perpetrator. She called me a predator. I don't understand, as most of these women are my friends. I'm supposed to kite to continue the group. I've no desire to be under her, but my friends are begging me to stay.

I ate supper alone until a woman came over and mentioned the LRC. She went there but couldn't complete it and was sent back here. Now she has to jam her time [the top number]. I gave her a smile and bundled up, grabbed my CD player, and hit the yard. It was super cold, "hair-freezing white" cold. I listened to music, but only for a bit because I kept getting strip-searched. I could barely move my limbs when I finally came in. The yard was closed early for the drug team to come into our cells and swab our hands.

I only received one letter, but it was from you. I know my day is coming when I won't receive any mail. I'm glad you wrote that your Christmas sucked. I wish it didn't, but I'm glad I wasn't alone. I pray I'm at Work Release next year. I don't know if I could survive another Christmas here.

Mrs. R said she went to Famous Dave's for Christmas. I got excited thinking about it, but then I got heavy. I can't go there. I can't go anywhere. It's not about the BBQ, as delicious as it is. It's the freedom to do things. I'm a prisoner. It's a difficult concept to grasp, so I choose not to think about it. It's worse when an unexpected happy memory comes, and realization stabs it to death.

December 28, 2007

There's a war raging inside me. I'm tired of this battle, and it's only begun. I need to fully trust. Just when I think I've got it, I'm flat on my face again. I want to give up and stay down. I ask Jesus to return and rescue me every day. I want to be with you, have children, and enjoy freedom, but it's just difficult and so long. Ephesians 6:13, "And having done all to stand." I feel like I'm just trying to stay on my feet. I'm not trying to dance, jump, skip, walk, or run. I just want to stand.

December 31, 2007

Happy New Year! We watched the Dick Clark special. I'm glad 2007 is over. Nicole got her Bible and loves it! I saw the truest smile sweep across her face. She looked through my Bible and read all my notes. She also got a letter from your grandmother, whom she loves and raves about. Daisy loves the present your sister sent her. I love the glittery Christmas cards. I put on a little glitter for an added glow for visits.

January 1, 2008

These women are so appreciative of the mail and encouragement your mom, grandma, and the women in their Bible studies have given them. They're starving for someone to care about them. I feel flickers of hope and light with every letter that's sent in. I've seen slow changes in Nicole. She's endured abuse both outside and inside this place. This past week she started coming to church with me. Growth here is slow. There's been much heartache and pain.

January 2, 2008

Lynn's out of Segregation. The head teacher told me to make sure she did all her work while she was gone. I'm not sure why I was assigned to her. That didn't go so well last time.

Lynn wasn't next to me for five minutes when she had another full-blown temper tantrum. It was worse than the one that sent her to Segregation. She slammed her fists down right in front of my face, nearly hitting me. The table shook, dumping my lemonade all over the books. I picked up her mess while she continued screaming. Finally, the head teacher told her to go to her cell. All the TAs were rattled up. This place is crazy!

Nicole wanted to share her brief story and prayer to post on our website.

Nicole's Letter for Our Website

My name is Nicole, and I'm a domestic violence survivor. I was in a violent relationship for ten years, to which I suffered a broken cheekbone, two broken ribs, a broken hand, and two miscarriages. He held a gun to my head and threatened to kill me. Unfortunately, this relationship tragically ended in the death of my husband. By the grace of the Lord, I'm alive today, but I'm serving 12 to 16 years for manslaughter. It was truly self-defense. Please pray for our children and my family. Thank you, and God bless.

Prayer for Justice and Mercy

Jesus, united with the Father and the Holy Spirit, give us Your compassion for those in prison. Mend in mercy, the broken in mind and memory. Soften the hard of hearts, the captive of anger. Free the innocent, parole the trustworthy. Awaken the repentance that restores hope. May prisoners' families persevere in love. Jesus, heal the victims of crime; they live with the scars. Lift the eternal peace to those who die. Grant victims' families the forgiveness that heals. Give wisdom to lawmakers and to those who judge. Instill prudence and patience in those who guard. Make those in prison ministry bearers of Your light, for all of us are in need of Your mercy. Amen.

January 3, 2008

While at school this morning, I was called to the A building. My heart sank. If you're called to A, something important is being delivered. Mrs. R said she's praying against LRC and will be here when I return. It was such a long walk. I prayed God would send ten thousand angels to accompany me. My heart raced wildly as I reminded myself to breathe.

I rang the buzzer. The head of Mental Health, who also runs SALSA, met me at the door. She escorted me to a chair and asked me to sit. I felt like a kid getting put into a time-out. She said I'm no longer allowed in the SALSA program because I'm a sex offender and considered a perpetrator. The other women are victims, and I'd hinder their growth. They'd identify me as their perpetrator, even if I've been a victim myself.

She asked if I'd heard from LRC. I said that's what I thought I was finding out. She smiled at me. I certainly didn't feel like smiling back. She said if I'm approved for LRC, I'll get what I need there. I quickly left.

I wish they would've told me when I signed up that I couldn't join. It would've saved time, hurt, and embarrassment. I felt the burden and pain of every woman, as if I'm to blame for what they've experienced. I feel unworthy to be in a group of any sort. I'm subhuman and don't deserve the opportunities others get.

I returned to school and tried to force it out of my mind. Mrs. R wanted to know, so I told her. She laughed, saying she was stressed and didn't want me to leave. I suggested she should call and tell them.

I started sinking into depression and cried out to God. He said, "What has changed?" I'm hurt for sure, but that's not new or something that won't return. I'm still in the same position. My label was thrown in my face again, making me want to sink, but I'm still in the same boat. I'm choosing to trust God even though it hurts so terribly much.

I told Mary I wouldn't be returning to SALSA. She angrily said it was ridiculous to say she'd ever see me as her perpetrator, as I'm nothing like her husband. She'd never trust him with anything, but she'd trust me with her life. Daisy ran up, freaking out, as she heard me being paged to A. She's also very upset with me getting banned. I'm relieved I don't have to do some program I don't agree with. I hurt, but I'm okay. God must've sent those ten thousand angels down.

When I got to my cell, Nicole was frantic with news. Terry's still convinced I turned her in for cheating. Nicole tried to help, but Terry wasn't making sense and told Nicole she was coming after me. Terry's a lifer for decapitating someone and has nothing to lose. She's been practicing witchcraft in the chapel and her cell.

I showered quickly with Mary standing guard. Showers are where women typically get jumped, and I'm trying to watch my back. After I got back to my room, Terry yelled down the hall, asking Nicole for my inmate number. Nicole told her, and Terry said, "Her nasty panties are on the floor in the bathroom." I quickly ran to get them. I get written up if I lose one article of clothing. The only reason I accidentally left them was that I was in a rush with Terry on the warpath. Mike, why is this happening?

Tonight was the first night I didn't receive mail. I'm thankful for the support I have, but I really needed encouragement. I received a returned check from JCPenny. They were out of several things I ordered.

I've never been this afraid of someone. I know I'm not to fear, but she's capable of awful things. She has spies everywhere. I feel lost for words, and I'm sinking once again. I don't want to appear weak, but I'm fighting to stay above water.

January 4, 2008

The teachers called me in when I got to school. They knew Terry has been threatening me, and I filled them in on last night. They warned that Terry is deeply involved with evil. They and the TAs believe it's because I'm a Christian that she's attacking me. I didn't tell the teachers that Terry lives across from me. If Terry attacks, I'm supposed to drop to the ground in a ball and take it. Oh, and pray a guard sees it.

My TA friend lives with her baby in the nursery. She keeps asking what's wrong. I'm trying to keep my mouth shut. She gets to go back to happy baby land, and I have to go back with the most violent criminals.

I haven't seen Nicole. I think she believes me, but she's very afraid of Terry. The last thing I need is Nicole teaming up with her old cellmate. Nicole and I were just starting to get along.

I'm glad I have a visit tonight and won't see her. She hasn't received a visit since I've been here. I do pity her. I'm trying not to hate her, but I'm struggling. Why would someone act like this? She must be filled with so much hate. I'm so tired right now. I may try to sleep during lockdown.

January 5, 2008

Terry glares at me with penetrating eyes as she walks by. I avoid eye contact, but I feel darkness that I've not felt before. Her eyes have changed. They seem more dark, raging, and dead set on me. I feel an evil presence. If I could lift the veil that keeps us from seeing the spiritual world, we'd be surrounded by a war waged by angels and demons. I'm scared, but I feel covered.

I was playing cards in the hall when Terry showed up at the next table. She tried to intimidate me by glaring at me. I saw her out of the corner of my eye but didn't make eye contact. Her intense eyes were fixed on me the entire time. Although I felt uncomfortable, I stayed and tried to have a good time.

Now I'm freaking out. Mary told Tinley about Terry coming after me. Tinley was the one across from me in Segregation. Your mother writes her. Tinley was hot, saying she'd take care of it. I took my shower while Tinley and Mary talked.

Later, Tinley called me into the shower. Terry was there and conjured up a lame apology. I said, "I'm not a snitch, and I didn't even know you cheated."

Terry said Nicole was lying because she was talking about another TA. That was a lie, but it satisfied Tinley, and we all left.

I went back into my room and filled in Nicole. Terry came to our door and said Nicole didn't lie; then, she admitted she did. Terry lied to Tinley to appease her. Terry stuck out her hand and said, "It's over." I shook her hand, and she left.

I'm thoroughly confused. Nicole said Tinley has pull with all the Black lifers. Terry has to deal with them since she has life. Tinley's on my side, and thus I have her friends' support.

I thank and praise God. God put me across Tinley's room not only here, but also in Segregation. Your mom writes Tinley, sending her encouragement, provision, studies, and a Bible. Tinley stood up for me and has several in her corner. I have no idea what'll happen, but I can at least breathe. God's delivered me this day.

January 7, 2008

It was a draining morning. Mrs. R said Terry wants a meeting with the TAs to erase the slate and "clear the spirit." I'm not sure what spirit she's talking about. Mrs. R wants me to put in a cell request so I'm not across from Terry. I laughed, as there isn't any "requesting" around here. The only way to change cells is to PC yourself, which I'm not doing.

Angry Woman couldn't set up a story problem if her life depended on it. She wants me to do her work. When she makes a mistake, she throws her pencil, eraser, or anything nearby. She angrily throws a forty-year-old temper tantrum. She always asks for help with just one more problem. It's never just one more. If I tell her it's been fifteen minutes, she gets mad and asks the teacher, who says it's fine. It's not fine; I've got a long line of students waiting.

I overheard Angry Woman say the TAs think they're cops and won't help. Seriously? Who helped you all morning? I don't want to be depressed. I'm constantly watching my back. There are so many of them at school. All the TAs are stressed. School was better before. I don't want to give up teaching, but is it worth this? God doesn't give us too much, but this is too much. Nicole told me to get a job change. I don't know if that's the only problem.

I walked instead of going to dinner. My stomach was upset, and I thought I was going to throw up. I'm anxious and paranoid. I can't keep the tears from stinging my eyes. I'm a mess. I went into the lobby to talk to Daisy. Terry and her gang sat at another table, and I felt the heat of their eyes. Daisy was told to watch her back.

I'll do another Bible study during the week. I should try every morning. It feels better when we're together. I won't go to church this Sunday or the last Sunday of this month. They don't preach the Bible, so I'm not going. I miss church. I'm dying here.

I just got mail. I received a letter from the LRC. Here are my results. My future is displayed before me on one sheet of paper. My hands are shaking, and I can't breathe.

CHAPTER 9

Accepted

I've been accepted into the LRC. It's too much. I feel numb. I'll call you first thing in the morning. Mikey, with all my heart, I don't want to go there. I feel like I'm breaking into several pieces and my life is being squeezed from me. Nicole is asking why I'm crying. She thinks it's about the men crying on the *Biggest Loser*. It'll be my copout.

They'll take me as soon as there's an open bed. How long is that? This is an awful day. Why would God want me to go there? I understand the words of David, "I want to die from my youth up" (Psalm 88:15). I have no words. I feel poison spreading over every inch of my body. I wish I wasn't alone right now. This feels like the hardest thing. Everyone will ask what's wrong. I'll bawl if I tell them. I'm such a mess.

I got a letter from you. You write about this great life we'll have after this. Yeah, real great after they screw me up. This life you speak of doesn't seem real and so far away. Can I make it through this? I don't think there's anything I can do. I'll have to go. If I refuse my program, then I'll be here years longer. Why'd they send a letter instead of talking me through it? I just want to go home.

January 9, 2008

I'm trying not to think about LRC in my lame attempt to get through today. I told Mrs. R, and she was upset. I've had a couple of breakdowns. God's in control, but it doesn't feel like it. I know He wants what's best for me, but I keep thinking about living in a sex offender mental institution for two years and start having panic attacks. I really don't want to go, but it's the fastest way home. There's no way I can do five to eight years.

I'm trying not to tell anyone. A couple of TAs mentioned I don't look well. They know my results are coming. School's getting worse. TAs are uncomfortable around students. There's been more harassing, belittling, antagonizing, and threats. I'm the only TA with language and math skills, so I'm the one they go to. We need bigger facilities. Half the battle is that everyone is physically too close—one TA is in Segregation after pushing a student, which leaves more work to do.

I walked until shower time. Mary guarded me. How did I get here? It's sad to think of my past life and all I left behind. I don't want to face what's to come. It's time to read my Bible.

January 10, 2008

My caseworker called me in, asking what I'd heard from LRC. It seems dumb that she asked because she already knew. A couple of beds opened. It's against policy to say when I'll be leaving, but sometime in the next couple of weeks. She said it was good I was accepted into the "road to recovery" and the fastest way home.

I explained the LRC is a two-year program. The judge said I'd get out in two years if I did well. It's already been three months, so I'm just adding time. She continued, saying that I needed to look at my bottom number of four years. My parole eligibility date says two years, but good time is not a guarantee, especially not with my charge. Then why would the judge say that? Why are my hopes crushed again, especially facing a mental institution? She said I wouldn't come back to prison unless I got kicked out of the program.

I asked basic questions about the LRC, and she didn't know. Oddly, she doesn't know much about a place she speaks so highly about. I'll find out when I get there. I hope I don't go through D&E for a month with no visits or calls, but I'm not getting my hopes up.

I got my things from JCPenney. I was so excited about my new stuff, but the excitement didn't last. I was paged back to Property. They said I leave on January 23rd. I get packed out on the 18th, so that's five days of wearing the same clothes. I don't think I can take my new clothes. I'm frustrated I can't get a straight answer.

I can't believe I will leave in a week and a half. People already know because inmates work in Property. I'm relieved to get out of this hall, but what am I trading it for? I don't know how to tell everyone. I feel ashamed I have to go there and am afraid to tell people. I know nothing about a place I'll live for two years.

God's giving me peace, which is nothing short of a miracle. I'm really trying not to worry. I keep focusing on the fact this is what I have to do to get home. Dinner was gross, so I walked instead. I saw Mary crying as she headed to dinner. She works in Property and saw my papers.

Mary said Cheyenne's going to the LRC as well. Cheyenne's been to my study a few times and writes your mother. She's been telling everyone she's going to Work Release. I don't blame her. I wonder if I'll be able to see her there. God has put her on my heart before.

Later, I played cards with Daisy and Mary. Daisy said she misses living with me. Her eyes lit up, and I felt it with her whole heart when she said, "I miss my Brandy." How can I tell her I'm leaving? Ruby walked by and said she saw me with my caseworker. She asked me what was going on. Daisy joined in. I told them it was about the school situation. Nicole walked up, saying, "I'm nosey. Why were you seeing your caseworker? Are they moving you? They better not move you."

I couldn't take it. I lied. Yup, sure did. God, please forgive me. I'll tell them before I go to Property. I won't avoid them. I want to enjoy our time and don't want it to be miserable. I have to be the tough one. Nicole desperately doesn't want a different cellmate. She's had awful cellmates who've abused her. Three of them I've had issues with.

All you have to do is get a new scarf, and you're famous in prison. I do have good taste, but I've never gotten this many compliments in my life. I wonder if Joseph felt like this with his coat of many colors. I hope I can take my new stuff with me. No one knows what I'm allowed. I won't be able to make money because I won't have a job. Going to treatment all day without working sounds terrible.

January 11, 2008

I went to breakfast with Daisy. Since we were alone, I decided to tell her on the walk back. She wanted to stop and look at me, but I urged her to keep walking. I think that helped. Then we headed to the lobby for Bible study. She was crying but not freaking out. Tears welled in my eyes. She told me not to cry; otherwise, she couldn't handle it.

No one else showed up for the study, so we talked and prayed together. She said she'd try to continue the study in my place. She kept emphasizing, "In your place." I think it helps keep her connected to me.

Christina got room restrictions for getting into it with a student. She put in for a job change and isn't the only one. At this rate, the school won't have any TAs left. The teachers reassigned my job. I wanted to cry. Now the TAs know I'm leaving, so it's a matter of time until everyone knows.

Grandma, Mom, and Kristy visited me. They asked questions about LRC, and I have no answers. Fears assail me, but I know this is where God leads. I can't wait to see you tomorrow.

January 13, 2008

Thanks for coming. When I got back, I told Nicole I was leaving. I've been sick about it, and the words popped out. I thought she'd be angry at me. A well of emotions released from her that felt like years of pain. She got out tears she'd been holding back for a while. It was a safe place to cry. She wants to make a going away feast for the two of us.

I spent some time with Daisy and Ruby tonight, encouraging them to continue what they've been learning. They should be going to Work Release about the same time. That makes sense because we all have similar sentences. Could you check into a good church they can go to?

I read the letter from your grandmother. It was encouraging and moved me to tears. She's a real encourager. I wish I could tuck her into my pocket and take her with me to the hospital.

January 14, 2008

My cramps are horrendous. It got worse throughout the day until I could barely function. I had stabs of pain shooting through my stomach. Everything irritates me, especially the whiney and discontent students. One girl I helped smelled like she hadn't showered in weeks. I thought I'd pass out. The cleaners came with a foreign cleaner that's unbearable to breathe. I'm so sick that I may vomit. I want to sleep.

Our new head teacher said she's very sad I'm leaving. It's probably because she doesn't know algebra and sends students to me. She said, "I've only known you a short time, but I know you'll do well and get it done soon. We never understand why these things happen, but we will in the end." That was nice.

Terry's on a thirty-day room restriction for tattooing herself. I'll be gone before she gets out. Happy dance! At Bible study tonight, Nicole announced to everyone that I'm leaving—so much for keeping this on the down low. It was difficult to concentrate after that. A few women asked where I was going. After I said LRC, they responded, "Wow, you have to go there? Oh, well, you'll be okay." How comforting. The words, "With God, all things are possible," kept coming to mind. I somehow felt worse after the study.

I wish I knew someone who'd already endured this. Someone who knows what lies ahead. I'll have to take my pictures off my bulletin board. Change is difficult. I'm a creature of habit. I wish I was leaving for home or Work Release instead. I wish you were here with me through this.

January 15, 2008

Nicole made burritos and invited a few friends for a little going away party. Daisy was distant and upset. She blamed the burrito. Nicole and I went back to our room as everyone else had to go to AA. I said goodbye to Cheyenne as she left for the LRC. I miss Taco Bell. I wish I could make a run for the border.

January 18, 2008

My dad came tonight, and it was good to see him. He definitely is uncomfortable with me being here and looks scared. *Me too, Dad!* He gave me a hard time for not calling more. I feel bad and am torn. I only get fifteen minutes a day.

There was a fifteen-year-old girl getting a visit. She was sentenced to life. I don't get how one fifteen-year-old is responsible for their actions, and the next fifteen-year-old is not. Her poor parents were shaking. I was saddened by the reality that I don't know when I'll see my dad again.

I received my Avon order, but had to pack it out. It's sad my new stuff is gone. I'm writing in the dark because my light is in Property. I have no book to get lost in. I did get to keep both Bibles, but I had to beg.

I can't wait to see you and your parents tomorrow. I'm glad they're there for you as I transition to Lincoln. I just realized my picture tickets are in my address book packed in Property. Daisy will be in Visiting since she's the photographer. She's dying to meet your mother. That was $4 for two pictures. That's like so much money here!

Nicole's really struggling with my leaving. She whines and cries every day. She said she doesn't like anyone but me in prison.

January 19, 2008

A woman named Becky walked up to me in the lobby before lockdown. She works in Property and asked about LRC. She revealed her doubts God is with her here. She hopes she'll do good things after prison to earn her way to Heaven.

My words flowed, "Becky, you don't have to be good enough. Christ is enough. You can know for sure you'll spend eternity with your Creator. You'll never have to work to earn it. We've all sinned and fallen short of a perfect God. God loved us so much that He sent His Son to die for us. If we confess our sins and believe He is Lord, He's faithful to forgive us and cleanse us. Only Jesus. Nothing more."

She closed her eyes and tears flowed as she invited Jesus into her heart. She asked Him to forgive her for all the wrong she had committed. She believed Christ died for her sin on the cross. She now has the power of the Spirit to strengthen her through this time.

When I went back to my room, Nicole asked me what had happened with Becky. She and Becky attend mass together and will be here for a while. This experience blessed me so much. It made my trip to prison worth it (gulp). Now it's really time to rest. Apparently, I wasn't finished with this day. To God be the glory!

January 22, 2008

We had a tough conversation this morning. I can't imagine how you're feeling about me leaving tomorrow. I feel like I let you down when I tell you I'm afraid. It's difficult to hear you say I'm not trusting God enough. Believe me; I'm trying!

I don't expect you to understand what I'm going through, just as I can't fully grasp what you're going through. What I need is to know when it gets tough, I can tell you how I'm feeling. Try not to let me know when you feel disappointed in my responses. This isn't easy, and I won't deal with it perfectly. Women in prison dread going where I'm going. It's another animal altogether. Please don't give up trying to encourage me after "Just trust God" isn't enough.

You told me you have nothing more to say. Pray God gives you the words to speak to me. God uses you to encourage me all the time. No one has the power to calm me as you can. I depend on you more than you know, so please don't give up on the conversation after a couple of Christian catchphrases or my bad attitude. Stick it out with me. I can't tell anyone else how bad things really are. My friends and family can't handle it like you can.

I'm sorry if I'm difficult and weak. I need you to be strong for me, just like you want me to be strong for you. Let's ask God to make us both strong in Him. He'll make you into what I need and me into what you need.

Now I need to rest. Tomorrow I leave this prison for the great unknown.

CHAPTER 10

Lincoln Regional Center

January 23, 2008

I was paged after the doors were unlocked and said goodbye to Nicole. Daisy and Ruby walked me up to Master Control. The tears wouldn't stop flowing, and their goodbye hugs couldn't be tighter. I watched them grow greatly in the three months I'd known them. They promised to continue the Bible study at York.

An officer met me and loaded up my trash bags. I got inside the vehicle, and we exited. I had to be handcuffed, which I'd expected, but it was uncomfortable. I hadn't been in a car in almost four months. It was surreal driving through the town and exiting on the highway. The officer was nice and asked me questions about the LRC. I had no idea what to tell him.

We pulled onto the campus with several buildings. The officer escorted me into a rundown building. We walked into what looked exactly like a mental ward in a scary movie. Everywhere I looked, there were chipped metal bars. All the metal was white and had been painted over multiple times. I silently freaked out as the officer went to the front desk.

He was told we were in the wrong building. The officer confessed he'd considered taking me back to York if that's where I'd stay. We finally found the correct building. I gulped as I entered an old brick building. I was released from the handcuffs and the officer left.

An older orderly introduced himself, saying he wasn't an officer, but was on staff. He was dressed in regular clothing and checked in all my items. Thankfully, most of the items I could keep. He showed me to the small lobby with the other three women in the unit. I saw Cheyenne, who was relieved to see me. She hasn't talked much to anyone. Ruth is the oldest, about 45, and is nice. I did a double take as I thought the final woman was a boy. Her name is Kelly, and she is young like me.

I was excited I had my own little room and bathroom. That was the best thing I saw all day. When I entered my room, I strangely felt cold and isolated. I unpacked my things until it was time for dinner.

I sat with Cheyenne. She's very unhappy here. I tried to cheer her up, saying the food was better and we can do our own laundry. After dinner, we headed back to the dayroom. We have to stay out of our rooms until 8 p.m. When we aren't in group, we must be in the dayroom. Cheyenne and I have to work up in levels before we can stay up later.

It's so quiet here, strangely quiet. I feel on edge. I have no idea what to expect in the sessions tomorrow, and I'm scared. Someone walks by our room every hour. They did at York too, but I never noticed as much in all the noise. Strange faces keep peeking through the window. I feel unsettled. It's been a long day, but I can't sleep.

January 24, 2008

I bawled myself to sleep last night. It was nice to have a room to myself, but I felt alone. I'd take my smelly cellmate back in a second. I miss not talking to you in the morning. Hopefully, you can bring in a phone card soon. I've had a terrible headache since I arrived.

I enjoyed having a job to make my days fly by. I hate sitting around all day. It reminds me of an old folks' home. The staff said it's too cold to go outside. My first group, called the SO [sex offender] group, is soon. Feel free to take me home at any time.

SO group went okay. The therapist, Dee, asked me to share as much as I wanted. I introduced myself, what I did, and that I take full responsibility for what I've done. The others introduced themselves and said why they were here. Cheyenne had a rough time talking. Dee said I did extremely well, and that Ruth has been here for years and couldn't top that intro. Ouch, I felt bad for Ruth.

Dee did my drug/alcohol evaluation afterward. It went quick as I rarely drink and haven't done drugs. She said I did amazing, which surprised her. My evaluation report from York said I didn't take much responsibility. I told her I did take responsibility and was honest. Dee seemed surprised I was here.

The other therapist for another group is Rita. Rita was one of the two women that interviewed me at York. She approaches issues differently. She said everything he did was my fault. I have to use terms like "forced, raped, and molested." That isn't the truth. I'm responsible, but that's not what happened. I'll have to be very careful with wording.

Thank you for bringing my stuff. I wish I could've seen you. I'm so thankful I don't have to wait a month to visit you like in York. That's a huge praise! I'll see you on Saturday.

I have to be in my room each day from 2:30 to 4 p.m. It's like lockdown, but we don't get locked in our rooms. I can't make money, but you can bring me things in. I can have burned CDs. When you come to visit me, you can bring food in. I can't believe it! I could so go for a steak! The food here isn't great, but it's a step up from prison.

January 25, 2008

I took several tests. The first was a psych evaluation. The woman who gave the test was quite the character wearing hip clothing, but composed herself like an older professor. She said it'd take an hour, but we finished ten minutes later. She said that's never happened, and I'm doing amazingly well.

Next was a personality test. Then the same horrendous 600-question sexuality test that I took that at the probation office before sentencing, and at York. I hate the wording and asked if he's considered a child. She said everyone asks her that. Twelve and under is considered a child. That question went against me in county because they considered fifteen a child. That's why they thought I'm not taking responsibility. That test is unclear and unreliable.

My mom and grandma finally arrived. Toward the end of my visit, Dr. Mann called me into his office. He wouldn't wait until my visit ended in ten minutes. Dr. Mann is the highest-paid psychiatrist in the state and very difficult to understand. I think he's Indian, but not sure. He recorded me, which was intimidating. He asked several questions and said he'd see me next week.

I was in tears when I got back to my family. Grandma was on the warpath and wanted to drop-kick everyone to the moon. I hushed her a few times. There are staff sitting in Visiting, but she certainly didn't care.

January 27, 2008

I got to see you today! I also got to talk to you not once, but twice on the phone! Thanks for the whopper, fries and goodies. I'm in heaven with my comforter and pillows. It feels a little like home. I just want to wrap myself in it all day long. I couldn't ask for more from my amazing husband. I'm so happy I see you again tomorrow. Please include the following letter for our website.

Letter for the Website

Thanks for praying for this transition. It's been difficult, and I've not adjusted, but God continues to walk me through each step. There's a large group of twelve on the treatment team, including a therapist, counselor, psychologist, psychiatrist, caseworker, social worker, and many other staff members that monitor us all day. It feels like every thought, motive, and action are monitored. I've taken several evaluations, interviews, and tests. I have several more, so pray God guides me.

The greatest way we can demonstrate Christ is to love others, not just by words, but by actions. York was a wake-up call, especially living in North Hall. There are some very unlovely women there. I'd already made the decision to show love no matter what they'd done, but some of these women had done horrible things.

God loves us unconditionally right in the middle of our crazy lives, running away from Him. That's why Christ died for us. We don't have to clean up our act in order for Him to love us. He wanted me to love these women in the middle of their storm. No one is beyond forgiveness. I was able to share God's love with women carrying sinful labels, much like my own.

James 5:20, "Let him know, that he which converts the sinner from the error of his way shall save a soul from death, and shall hide a multitude of sins." I praise God for allowing me to lead a woman to Him three days before I left. It confirmed this verse in my mind.

January 28, 2008

More tests today and tomorrow. I have my TPR [Treatment Program Review] on Wednesday. I'll be in a room with a treatment team of twelve people and will receive my program. I'm a bit intimidated but was told I won't have to say anything.

We had Relapse Prevention [RP] with Rita. It went fine because Cheyenne had her teeth pulled, and we didn't cover much without her. This group helps identify thoughts and behaviors that led to our crime and how to avoid similar situations again.

Poor Cheyenne is in lots of pain and can't eat. Could you get her a Bible? She's quiet and has much bottled up inside. I'm concerned about her. I love you.

January 30, 2008

I had my TPR today. The team of twelve and I met in a small, crowded room. Dr. Mann asked extremely personal questions in front of everyone. He asked why I loved Todd. I tried to explain the emotional attachment that developed over time during the hours in the car each day. He didn't seem satisfied with my answer. He wanted to know why this specific young man. I didn't know, except that he did all the things I wanted you to do. He told me to think about it and made me leave.

They stayed in the room for over an hour. I went to my room, and the tears flowed for a long time. I didn't even know half the people in there. The questions were fired at me like I was under attack. I'm glad it's over, but I'll have to do this each month. My heart's still beating out of my chest.

I told the women about my TPR and how Dr. Mann asked me question after question. They were shocked as they were never asked any questions at their TPR.

January 31, 2008

A group of nursing students came with their instructor. We have to share why we're here. They ask whatever questions they want. It's difficult to be open with complete strangers. Dr. Rita listened to our responses. I felt so much pressure and dread at the next batch coming.

I did a Bible study with Cheyenne with Dr. Rita watching from the bubble. It was a challenge with the other two talking and watching TV. In the words of Tinley, "Sleep with the angels."

February 2, 2008

You're the highlight of my weekend. Our time together recharges my batteries for another week of therapy. It's crazy where our marriage is today and how far we've come. There were a few times I wanted to walk away, but I couldn't do it. Even at our worst, I still had hope. Our marriage hasn't been pretty. It's been attacked, but pushing through made our marriage stronger. If we put each other first, we'll endure the stabs this world tries to inflict on our family. God has to be our rock, center, foundation, and on the throne of both our hearts.

I believe God picked you to be my husband. I'm proud of you for getting another job, taking care of the dogs, cleaning, paying bills, coordinating visits, making the website, visiting me, bringing me what I need, and going to church. I'm looking down at my Superman shirt. That's what you are, a Super Man, or Super Mike, I should say. I pray that God protects our marriage and keeps you from falling into temptation.

I know I've said this before, but I'm sorry for the terrible wife I was. I should've never cut off communication with you despite how wounded I was. I closed our door and opened another. It was a dark path that led me down a devastating road. "Sin will take you further

than you wanted to go, keep you longer than you wanted to stay, and cost you more than you wanted to pay."

February 8, 2008

Cheyenne was quiet during group, until the end. She hates living in a box and wants to snap. She said she's liable to hurt people and will look for objects to use. I hope she's trying to sound worse in group, but she has a violent past. If I say anything she doesn't agree with, she just stares at me.

Part of me wants her to go back, if that's what she wants. She's angry and complains all day, which gets me down. If she goes back, she may tell people about the things I've shared. I've openly talked about my past and about Terry, whom Cheyenne was friends with.

I get upset with myself because God created Cheyenne and loves her. He wants her to know Him and have a relationship with her. Right now, I easily offend her. We didn't get together yesterday. We still sit together at meals, but I can't read her and feel like I'm walking on eggshells.

My social worker said women stay here for two years. Kelly passed her parole eligibility last month. She sees the board next month in hopes she can start transitioning home. The whole process tacks on another year, so a year past her parole.

I just saw Dr. Mann. He asked about my two biggest problems. I had written down "worry" and "boundaries." He was upset because I talked to Dee about my assignment and accused me of getting help. I told him I didn't ask for answers. I just told her what I was working on. She said she couldn't talk about it, so I dropped it. I didn't realize I'm not to talk about assignments.

He was upset that I wrote down my answers, but that's what he told me to do. There's no pleasing this man. He said I didn't come to a mental institution to work on "worry." Prison takes care of that.

I thought, "All you work on in prison is trying to survive!"

He then asked about boundaries. I tried explaining, but he cut me off, "'Boundaries' is not why you're in a mental institution." Yep, he used those words.

He hated everything that came out of my mouth. I remained calm, though I felt like I was on fire. Everyone writes down everything I say. They ask for my thoughts and feelings, but use them against me. I told Kelly about my meeting afterward. She said she had "worry" as one of her answers, and he accepted it. Seriously.

February 9, 2008

I'm still upset about my meeting. It's spiraled into fear. When I don't tell them what they want to hear, it prolongs my stay. I'm especially afraid of displeasing Dr. Mann, for he has the final say to release me.

I started with devotions. The subject was submission and resting in God's reality. The challenge at the end was, "What do you have to submit before you can rest?" My answer was "worry and fear." Matthew 10:16, "Behold, I send you forth as sheep in the midst of wolves: be ye therefore wise as a serpent." Let's face it, I'm pretty naïve, and I don't know what to tell these people besides the truth. Verses 19–20 say, "But when they deliver you up, take no thought of how or what ye shall speak: for it shall be given you in that same hour what ye shall speak. For it is not you that speaks, but the Spirit of your Father which speaks in you."

I pray for words to speak in every situation. I submit myself to Him and share what He wants me to say. Should it shock me they don't always like it? The real kicker came in verses 28–32, "And fear not them which kill the body, but are not able to kill the soul, but rather fear him which is able to destroy both body and soul in hell."

I keep thinking I have to perform. I'm fearful when they don't like my answers because I'm trying to please them. God is ultimately in control and will release me when He wants, even if it feels like it's

Dr. Mann. God loves me more than I know. He knows what I need, even if I don't.

February 13, 2008

I'm nervous about my TPR next week. Here I go again. I keep praying, but it's like I go into default mode, and my brain starts rolling and takes over. I'm thinking about what I'll say, what their reactions will be, and how to adjust to their disappointments. I have therapy with Dee, and my stomach is in knots. I can't do this on my own strength.

Ben is one of the techs and nicknamed me "The Cheerleader." He asked Kelly if she's ever had fantasies of cheerleaders. He's done stuff like this before, but tonight, it's worse. I would've left the room if I had the option. I don't understand half the sexual innuendoes. Kelly takes much of the garbage, but she'll transition out soon. Apparently, my foot starts twitching when he talks, which makes it worse.

I talked to Pastor today. Hearing him talk of consequences I'll endure for the rest of my life hurts. Just writing about it makes my throat swell and my eyes overflow with tears. What kind of life is that? I know I screwed up really big, but now it's almost like I've ruined every chance I had for serving the Lord.

I've cut off every limb. I can't teach children. I can't even be around children for the next two years or more. I just want to be normal again. I think I'll have to wear the scarlet letter on my chest for a very long time. I'm alone except for this sad piece of paper to write upon.

Do we really want to have children? I'll be on probation. Is it wise to be a registered sex offender felon with small children? What about them going to school? They'll get picked on if that's even a possibility. I feel like I've ruined everything for everyone.

If this were my cross to bear because I was suffering for a good cause, it'd be different. I don't think I'd tremble as much with the weight of it, but it's my sin to bear. I know Christ bore my sin on the cross, so I shouldn't pick it up. It's difficult when it stares you in the face every day. My past casts a long, dark shadow on my entire future.

February 14, 2008

Happy Valentine's Day. Thanks for sending me a card. You talk about me being this amazing woman. I don't feel that at all. I feel weak, but you think I'm strong. I needed to hear your love and encouragement. Your belief in me makes me stronger.

I definitely struck it rich with ten letters today. The staff calls it my "fan mail." I'm blessed with amazing people who love me. Your mom said Daisy struggled when I left and isn't doing well. Ruby was upset with her for skipping Bible study. They should be going to Work Release soon. Your mom is writing fifteen women there.

February 16, 2008

My caseworker said there's a bill that'll likely pass. It'll reconstruct the sex offender registry. Currently, there are three levels. Level I is the least likely to re-offend, Level II is medium risk, and Level III is the greatest risk to society. I'm a Level I and will need to register for five years according to the current law.

If this bill passes, that all changes. I'll register much more than five years. Some states make you put a sign in your front yard and won't allow you to live or work within a certain radius of a school or daycare. Anyone who has already finished registering will have to re-register. No one gets grandfathered in.

She said I'm a unique case because I know I did wrong and am open to sharing everything and admitting fault. She asked me if prison helps us register correctly. I told her I didn't know.

February 20, 2008

I had a dream. A woman was released from prison and wanted to get her children back. Someone from church was outraged by the thought of that. The woman accepted Christ in prison and made great changes. I suggested someone help her with accountability, support, structure, life skills, parenting skills, and Bible study.

I kept throwing ideas out like wildfire. The woman from church was upset and left. I spoke about women receiving second chances. I volunteered to help the mother. If she did well, she slowly got her children back in monitored settings. Weird dream, but I felt led to write it down. I'm sure it's already implemented.

Ben drives me crazy by asking me questions about the news. He watched a story about a teacher caught with five different students and received the same sentence as me. Ben wants to pick this to death. I'm so ready for bedtime.

February 21, 2008

The nursing students just left. I hate when they come. Dr. Rita was in the bubble observing everything. When we finished, she said, "Now, was that so bad?"

I thought, "Really? You try being an open book for any question while being monitored. The length in a mental institution depends on it."

Then I met Dee. She often stares into my eyes, which has always been comfortable for me. She penetrated my heart when she said, "When I look at you and this entire situation you've walked through, it's difficult for me to swallow."

Time to rest. We have our big move to the new unit tomorrow.

CHAPTER 11

Level Up

February 22, 2008

For the Website

We've completed our move to the new unit. The greatest blessing is there are two-day rooms. One is the quiet dayroom where I can read without distractions. I no longer have to watch whatever my peers are watching.

Amos 3:2–3, "Can two walk together, except they be agreed?" Sin puts a brick wall between God and those around us. I think about my life when I walked in sin. I convinced myself I was okay because I taught in a Christian school and went to church. I tried to repent when the sin came, but continued what I was doing. I was a prisoner more than I am now. I'm in prison, but no walls are up. God tore them down.

I often feel like my life is wasting away. I think of things I'd be doing for God on the outside. God asks me, "What's a wasted life?" Reading His word, learning lessons, and living the life He directs isn't wasted time. Weight has lifted, and I take a deep breath. I don't always feel this way, but it's about truth. When truth sets in, you are free. When my feelings get involved, I often get disoriented. I feel alone and rejected, but am I? No, the truth is God is here.

I'd like to encourage others to learn from my mistakes and not continue living in sin. Don't go down that road or let go of God's hand. Hang onto God with every fiber of your being. Work to love Him more today than yesterday. Get to really know Him. Read His word and hear His voice above all others, for it'll strengthen you. Pray your heart out because your life depends on it.

February 26, 2008

I was studying the transfiguration of Christ in Luke, where God revealed His glory. We grow comfortable with the Christ we know. God continues to shatter the box I've put Him in. I can relate to the disciples who declare, "Who is this man!?" Christ brings us to places that force us to readjust our vision of Him.

While being here, I got to a point where I felt like I didn't know God at all. I didn't feel close to Him because of it. But the harder the winds have blown, the more I've taken root in Him. In the difficult times, I searched the Bible more. I'm here to learn and grow in Him. God arranged my surroundings to change my perspective of Him.

Mike, remember your priority is keeping yourself and your family grounded in God. Consider letting go of the second job if you're too tired to go to church or read your Bible. I see a difference when you seek Him first. We fell far when we didn't put God first in our lives and marriage. If we don't have time, we must make time. We only know the direction for our lives when we communicate with Him every day. We can't make it without Him. Just step back, evaluate, and make the decision God wants. I had no idea this would come out when I started writing.

March 2, 2008

You tell me to ignore people and not think about what they say. It feels foreign to me. I'm more sensitive than you, which is a great quality for a sex offender. It makes a difference how close I am to the person. It's easier to ignore strangers than someone close to me. "People in glass houses shouldn't throw stones." I try not to throw stones, because I don't want one thrown at me.

Becoming less sensitive requires some desensitizing. Hearing awful words and responses and not taking it to heart is a struggle for me. I don't believe it's something anyone signs up for.

I wish I'd stop crying and come to the great realization that I'm not going home tonight. I'm here by myself. Homesickness is like an illness, and there should be some medicine you can take. I feel sick every night. I don't know how much one can take. It makes sense there are many cold women in prison. It hurts too much to feel. Goodnight.

March 3, 2008

Mondays are rough with lots of groups and meetings. SOs are the most difficult. She said to consider the amount of "pleasure" versus the length of the sentence. I get it; you reap what you sow. Then she directed the next comment at me and said, "You're in it for the long haul." I felt the hope inside me crush. Our next assignment is to make a collage of ten things that happened prior to the crime.

I feel discouraged and depressed that my life is a waste. We cover so much heaviness. Where's the hope or encouragement?

These negative thoughts keep plaguing my mind. I hear her voice: "You're in it for the long haul." It's heavy, like chains weighing me down, taking away my breath.

I thank God I get to exercise afterward. Worship refreshes, renews, and reminds me to get my eyes back on Christ. It changes me from the inside out and allows me to hear God. I also listen to the "Unshackled" recordings your dad burned onto a CD for me.[6] It gives me the hope and encouragement I desire. These investments are eternal and I appreciate them greatly.

March 11, 2008

I've been reading about Rahab, the harlot. She's the first woman listed in Matthew's genealogy of Christ, which was every woman's dream. She's in the great hall of faith. God chose her because His ways are not our ways.

I wondered why the Bible kept calling her "Rahab the harlot." Moses and David were both murderers, so why weren't they labeled next to their crimes? She messed up, but why was she labeled "the harlot?" A branding to bear for life. I relate, with "sex offender" next to my name. It reminds us of where she was when God called her. God chooses the most unlikely people to accomplish His purpose.

I bet after she left and lived with the Israelites, they wouldn't let her forget her past. Even if they stopped the gossip and looks, I bet she never forgot. I'm sure she suffered with memories that haunted her at night. The most difficult time is at night while I'm all alone.

Her heavy label didn't hold her back. She's the mother of Boaz, who was noted for his integrity and character. It speaks volumes

---

[6] "True Stories That Make You Face Yourself and Think.," Unshackled, accessed May 17, 2023, https://unshackled.org/.

about how she lived after God changed her. She became an amazing mother and allowed God to use her despite how she sinned. I plan to do that as well. God has shown me a purpose. I can be used if I trust and hope in Him.

March 12, 2008

A song Elvis sang is running through my head, except I see Grandpa singing with his soothing voice, "Are you lonesome tonight? Do you miss me tonight?" Sometimes I wonder if my heart could actually break. I look at pictures from our Dells vacation. I experienced such inner turmoil. You couldn't see it by the smile on my face. I try to recapture every moment, joy, smile, and closeness. I wish I could've stored it in a jar to take out and experience in moments like this.

Why does it all hurt so much? I feel waves of sadness sweep over my body, sending deep shocks. I try to hush my sobs at night. Just when things seem to get a bit better, my heart goes down for the count once again.

I feel attacked. I'm questioned every time I go into the quiet room to do my Bible studies. If a smile isn't on my face, then I'm not adjusting and doing poorly. Almost every other day, new faces tour our facility. I'm an open book for all to read—a guinea pig trapped in a cage, required to jump when zapped.

Your words gave me a spark of motivation. You said you cannot live without me. I often feel I'm a lost cause, but God said I'll rise again. Beauty will somehow come out of this death. It's just I have so far to travel. I have to take it day by day. I cry to God for deliverance, knowing He can work a miracle. I don't think that's His will, which scares me. I'd love to go straight home, no York, no Work Release, no parole, just home.

Micah 7:7–9, "As for me, I look to the LORD for help. I wait confidently for God to save me, and my God will certainly hear me.

Do not gloat over me, my enemies! For though I fall, I will rise again. Though I sit in darkness, the LORD will be my light. I will be patient as the LORD punishes me, for I have sinned against him. But after that, he will take up my case and give me justice for all I have suffered from my enemies. The LORD will bring me into the light, and I will see his righteousness."

March 17, 2008

I shared how Todd's mother came to support me at my sentencing and how she wanted to visit. Dee said that says a lot about me because it's highly unusual for a victim's mother to want to see the perpetrator. Dee also said her minister preached something I'd mentioned last week. We talked about sensitivity, and I shared that the shortest verse in the Bible is "Jesus wept" (John 11:35). This connection seemed to impact Dee.

After groups, I dived into my Bible. It's vital we put God first and glorify Him. That's why He created us. In everything I do, I need to ask myself, "Does this bring glory to God?" If not, I need to get rid of it.

Recognizing and ridding myself of sin the moment it creeps in is key. I'm able to recognize attacks when I'm alone with the Lord. Sometimes, He brings a thought or action to mind that I need to surrender. Reading Scripture guides me to uproot anything not pleasing to God and ultimately against me.

I'm memorizing Galatians 1:10, which asks if we're pleasing God or people. If I seek to please people, then I'm not a servant of God but of others. I struggle with the need to please those determining the length of my stay.

April 12, 2008

Mark 10:28–30, "Then Peter began to speak up. "We've given up everything to follow you," he said. "Yes," Jesus replied, "I assure you that everyone who has given up house or brothers or sisters or mother or father or children or property, for my sake and for the Good News, will receive now in return a hundred times as many houses, brothers, sisters, mothers, children, and property—along with persecution. And in the world to come eternal life." We are doing God's will.

In verse 30, Jesus lists rewards for those who give things up for Jesus. One is persecution. If we live right, we will suffer. Persecution is our glory and gives God glory. Persecution equals glory. Our purpose in life is to accept Christ and glorify God. How do we glorify God? Persecution. We glorify God because of what we've left behind. I think of times my persecution led to reward.

Lamentations chapter 3 is powerful! Here's some from my Life Recovery Bible, "I am the one who has seen the afflictions that come from the rod of the Lord's anger. He has led me into darkness, shutting out all light. He hath turned His hand against me again and again, all the day long. He has walled me in, and I cannot escape. He has bound me in heavy chains. And though I cry and shout, He has shut out my prayers. He has blocked my way with a high stone wall; he has made my road crooked. He shot his arrows deep into my heart. My own people laugh at me. All day long, they sing their mocking songs. He has filled me with bitterness and given me a bitter cup of sorrow to drink … Peace has been stripped away, and I have forgotten what prosperity is. I cry out, 'My splendor is gone! Everything I had hoped for from the LORD is lost!' The thought of my suffering and homelessness is bitter beyond words. I will never forget this awful time, as I grieve over my loss. YET, I still dare to hope when I remember this: The faithful love of the LORD never ends! His mercies never cease. Great is His faithfulness; His mercies begin afresh each morning. I say to myself, 'The LORD is my inheritance; therefore, I will hope in him!'

The LORD is good to those who depend on him, to those who search for him. So it is good to wait quietly for salvation from the LORD. And it is good for people to submit at an early age to the yoke of his discipline ... For no one is abandoned by the LORD forever. Though He brings grief, he also shows compassion, but of the greatness of His unfailing love. For He does not enjoy hurting people or causing them sorrow..."

It's comforting to know you're struggling too. I often feel alone in this. When I hear how you feel weak, it reminds me we're all humans. You help me, even if all you do is listen. I want to do the same for you and be there as much as I can. We need to share our needs with each other to strengthen our marriage. It's when we don't share and communicate we run into problems. I may be hurting as well, but I will not break.

April 14, 2008

Today, we talked about core beliefs. Dr. Rita asked Kelly if she thinks women are dishonest as a whole. Kelly said, "Yes."

Rita asked if she could think of any women that were honest.

Kelly, staring straight at me, said, "Brandy."

Rita asked if there was anyone else she knew. Kelly replied, "Oh, yeah, and you, Rita."

I felt this was a positive step. I often get discouraged that I never get through to her. Kelly is bitter at God.

April 29, 2008

Cheyenne's struggling more. She shared that the past several nights, she's had a reoccurring dream: someone annoys her to the point she beats them up. It takes five people to stop and sedate her. If you say her name, she literally freaks out.

Kelly read me a poem she'd written about the last day she saw her father before he took his life. She explained how he slowly let the light go out into his empty shell. She described him being tormented by demons until he told her goodbye on her last visit with him. The tears fell from my eyes. How terribly sad to lose your father that way while locked up. He passed shortly before I arrived.

The new woman in the unit is Tess, and she gave full details on her crime today. It was pretty gut-wrenching. Kelly said she was going to throw up. Tess was vague about some questions she was asked. Dee raked her over the coals. This was not a mutual relationship, as she played a seducer to a much younger victim. Tess glares when someone tells her things she needs to work on.

Cheyenne was excited to give her assignment that she worked hard on. When Dee told her it needed extra work, Cheyenne became angry and defensive. Dee continued, "It must be difficult to share an assignment right after Brandy. Brandy just wows me after everything she does. It all just clicks for her."

My eyeballs about fell out of my head as I thought, "Thanks, Dee, please direct her anger toward me."

Cheyenne told her she was so mad that she wanted to hit someone. Dee said, "Well, hit Brandy; she's right next to you."

Surprisingly, Cheyenne opened up to me a little tonight. I'm praying about mentioning the Bible study. She asked me a couple of weeks ago but hasn't said anything about it since. I heard this quote, and I'm praying it's fulfilled: "Trusting God can turn a crisis into a treasure."

May 2, 2008

Psalm 23:5 says, "Thou anoint my head with oil; my cup runneth over." Just as the shepherd anoints a sheep's head with oil to keep the bugs from driving it insane, I pray God anoints and protects me from those around me.

After reading that this morning, I walked into the dayroom to all my peers intently staring at me. Kelly said, "Brandy, we have a question for you." I took a big gulp as she continued, "We're wondering why you're so happy all the time."

The words popped out, "God makes me happy."

I'm not happy all the time. I was experiencing the second part of the verse I read earlier, "My cup runneth over." I'm thankful for the precious love God pours into my heart and life each day. He really does it, even in the worst of circumstances. Somehow, I feel it more here than I ever did outside these walls. I long for you, my family and friends, and my puppies. I know God wants me here right now, and today, I'm okay.

I'm reading *The Bumps Are What You Climb On* by Warren Wiersbe.[7] He talks about how joy and love are the two shortest commodities in our world today. Most people are hungry for being both joyful and loved. As believers, we are to be filled with God's Spirit and power. When we are filled, others notice our attitude and actions. It's a great opportunity to demonstrate the difference Christ makes in a life fully rooted in Him.

I thought about what Kelly said to me, "Why are you happy all the time?" It isn't happiness they see; it's joy. Joy can make us happy, but there's a difference. Happiness is determined by our circumstances. If life is good, we are happy, but if our situation changes, we are unhappy. Joy is deeper. Joy isn't created by circumstances on the outside; it's the result of conditions on the inside. If we search for joy, we'll never find it. If we surrender to God, joy comes into our heart.

Wiersbe says, "Unsaved people might even create some problems for us to see what we will do." That is exactly what happened this

---

[7] Warren W. Wiersbe, *Bumps Are What You Climb on: Encouragement for Difficult Days* (Grand Rapids, MI: Baker Book House, 2006).

week. It's as if Satan himself said, "Happy you say, I can fix that." It's good that the other book I'm reading is on spiritual warfare, and I have been putting on my armor each day.

I'll leave you with my favorite quote from Wiersbe: "God does not judge a man's life on what the newspapers say. He judges righteously on the basis of what's eternal." Amen to that!

May 12, 2008

I love our time together. You made me feel special yesterday. You're so tired from working two jobs, so I told you to rest and stay home. You were adamant, saying our time is what gets you through, and you wouldn't miss it for anything. I would've understood if you stayed home, but you were determined. Your words revealed your heart and made mine soar.

I'm thankful you shared about temptations. I can't imagine how much you get tried each day. Thinking about the ways Satan tempts you is overwhelming. It isn't easy to hear. The old me wants to worry, fear, and panic, but I'd allow Satan victory. I pray for protection and for God to guard our hearts and minds.

The Bible says if we're not in the word and praying each day, we will fail. It motivates me to be intentional. We must never give up the fight. Satan's number one attack in a believer's life is family. Please keep your guard up. We aren't above anything.

Thank you for writing to me. Even if it's short, it means so much. Your mom writes that we should move to Illinois and start a prison ministry someday. She's in her sweet spot, writing and praying with these women.

I'm getting extra assignments since I'm ahead. It's a huge packet on transitioning out. I think it's for people who are leaving. I'm not quite sure why I'm going through this now, but I'm ahead, and it's a lot of information.

May 17, 2008

I'm sitting outside in the sunshine with a huge smile on my face. Thank you for the picnic lunch and the marriage books you brought. It's challenging to work on our marriage apart, but the time invested will be rewarded.

When thoughts of you leaving me enter my mind, I surrender them to God. I'm sure you have unwanted thoughts enter as well. If you ever need to talk, I'm here. I never want to be where we were before. I want to continue our communication and growth. I pray our marriage gets better with the passing of time.

May 24, 2008

I just received my TPR scoring. I received a Level II. When Level III is achieved, the team discusses transitioning out. There's a big point difference between hitting II and almost to Level III. My score was almost III. I jumped drastically from my first TPR. My next TPR is at the end of June.

I had questions about why a few areas were lower. Dee looked me in the eye and sighed, "We don't have people like you end up here. We want to give it time and make sure it's for real. We have no doubts, but it takes time. You've only been here four months. We're in no hurry to send you back to that awful place."

Dee explained I can learn from peers and staff. She gave me a time limit helping my peers with homework. I must address this limit with my peers to work on my assertiveness and boundary skills.

I'm shocked she mentioned the possibility of going back to York in hopes of Work Release. They've never said that was an option. Once inmates complete treatment, they're not supposed to return to prison. That's what all the caseworkers said.

I don't qualify for Work Release until September 24th. LRC's a much better living environment than prison. There are many fights at York and talk of institutional lockdown. If that happened, I'd be locked in my room without walking, working, church, or Bible studies. I'm much closer to family here. York is twice the distance away. I have more time to study my Bible here. My prayer is I arrive back to York at the exact time I need, to get to Work Release and not get stuck.

Today marks eight months I've been locked up. I've done four months at York and four here. I'm a third of the way if God answers my prayer and I'm able to get first parole eligibility. This would be nothing short of a miracle.

Kelly shared in group that she thinks she's a "lost cause." I'm surprised, as she seems so confident. I asked why she thought that. She said years ago, in youth group, she was acting up, and the youth pastor said, "There isn't any hope for you." She wants to get a tattoo that says, "Lost." The words escaped from my lips before I could blink, "Jesus came to save that which was lost. He came to save the least and loved them greatly."

I knew this was an opportunity to give the truth where she'd normally reject it. The greatest commandment is, "Love God with all your heart, with all your soul, and with all your mind," but He didn't stop there, "The second commandment is equally important, "Love others like you would yourself" (Matthew 22:36). There are no exceptions. I'm to love others as I love God. Others may not be living their life like they should, but it doesn't matter.

Later, Kelly sat putting a puzzle together. I asked if I could tell her something, and she nodded. The words flowed from my heart, "I'm very sorry Christians didn't respond the way they should've. I love you, and something tells me that you haven't heard that enough." Tears quickly filled her eyes as she nodded but didn't say a word.

I haven't met one woman that wasn't desperately hungry for love. Underneath, they all scream the same thing, "Someone, love me!" What if we loved others like we were supposed to? John 13:34–35 says, "A new commandment I give to you, That you love one another; as I have loved you, that you also love one another. By this shall all men know you are my disciples, if you love one another." I stare at a magnet I read every morning before I start another day. It reads, "Now these three remain, faith, hope, and love. But the greatest of these is love" (1 Cor. 13:13).

CHAPTER 12

Homesick

June 1, 2008

You just left, and I already miss you dearly. I know you're in a rut. I feel it too, but all I can say is my joy seriously comes from God. He promises to draw near to us. There's no other reason I have joy in my heart. I have no control over anything I do. I'm alone and do the same thing every day. I repeat in detail my sin that's examined under a microscope. There's no reason I'm pushing through, except God.

John 16:33, "These things have I spoken unto you, that in me ye might have peace. In the world ye shall have tribulation: but be of good cheer, I have overcome the world."

Some of my greatest encouragement came from you. You said, "The easy thing would be to run from God, but you didn't. God will use you greatly for your faith in Him. He has plans for you. It might not be an easy road, but being in God's will is where we find true joy." You were dead on. I hope you find comfort in your own words as I have. And, baby, we'll need to hear them again.

For the Website

I love hearing from you, so please keep the mail coming. My peers and staff call it "Brandy's Fan Club." You fuel me up to get through this valley. This is God's gracious hand of provision for me. I wouldn't be able to endure without your support. Staff must document how much mail I receive, since they document everything. The doctors talk about how much support I have and how unusual it is. You're a testimony. God goes beyond every length to demonstrate His love for me. We have to trust God, no matter what we go through and wherever His path may lead. We must hold His hand tightly, however scary the road gets. He'll never let go.

I had my monthly visit with the psychiatrist. It was rough, but God got me through it. I always wish I would've said things differently. I put too much pressure on myself. Please pray for these important meetings that determine my outcome. Thank you for all you do for me. Seriously, from the bottom of my heart, I love you all so very much.

June 8, 2008

I'm crying as I write. I miss you so much my body hurts. You just left from visiting. I feel actual intense pain in my heart as if it may burst. It feels like I'll be in this mental institution forever. When will this end? How is it I feel good one minute and break down the next? I know God is here, but today I cannot feel Him. I feel cold and numb, and it scares me. I'm just not this strong.

I know God says He'll answer all of our prayers. Often the answer isn't "no," just "not now." I must wait. I don't know if I can sustain under the pressure. I can't see how any good will come out of all this. I know He has a plan, but why all of this? God's all-powerful, so why couldn't He keep me from all this and still use me?

I was full-out surrendered to Him a year prior to my sentencing. I confessed everything and did all I could, and it wasn't enough. Here,

I have to relive everything under a microscope day in and day out. Where is grace? Where is forgiveness? Where is forgetting the past and moving on? Where is life? My life feels like it's on hold. I'm trapped like a guinea pig, subject to everyone's invasive comments, questions, and judgments—no physical or often mental privacy.

I want to go outside and run. Run so hard and fast I feel my chest heaving. I'd let the tears fall. All I want to do is call you, but if I walk up for the phone, everyone will see my tears and ask a million questions, which will turn into a group discussion. I pay dearly with unpacking all my thoughts, feelings, and emotions.

June 9, 2008

It was a terrible night. I've not cried that hard since I've been here. I wanted you to hold me and tell me everything would be okay. I remain in this locked tower. To make things worse, after pouring my heart out to God and asking for pleasant dreams, I had awful dreams about you leaving me. I overslept and didn't hear my alarm, which literally alarmed you. I try to be strong, but I am overwhelmed. I feel I'm failing you and should be able to do this. In my struggle, I let you down.

God gave me the strength to get through the long day of groups. In RP, we talked about how much we dislike prison. I'll go back through fire if it means getting to you faster. I received your letter, and I cling to your words of encouragement. I'll sleep with it under my pillow and pray the words sink into my brain.

After a nap, I exercised and listened to the Casting Crowns. My sister is coming this weekend, and we're doing a Bible study together. I wish I had a church to go to here. We don't go to any studies or church. I miss being around believers.

Next week is my TPR. I worry about time moving from one level to the next. God's in control, even when I panic and worry. I let worry, fear, and doubt back in through the door of homesickness. I bet you get this on our anniversary. Sigh, what a great anniversary gift, my depression. I know this will be behind us one day, and that's what keeps me going. I love you more than I ever have. Don't give up on me. Please love me through it.

For the Website

I pray you are well. Severe weather seems to be the norm. We've had several tornado warnings and taken shelter in the damp basement of this old brick building. Cheyenne's very afraid of storms. We get stuck down there for a while. The story of the three little pigs came to mind. I told the story with great expression and reinforced the end. The pigs lived because the wolf couldn't blow down the third pig's house. They were in a solid brick building, just like ours. A smile finally broke across her face, and she felt better.

Summer has hit hard. Homesickness returned and constantly dampens my spirit and slowly seeps into everything. I often think of all the things I'd be doing if I weren't here. Then I think of how different my life will be when I finally return as a registered sex offender. Fear sets in. All I want is for Mike to hug me and tell me it's all going to be okay, but reality screams that I'm alone, and the homesickness sets in again. The vicious cycle continues to repeat itself.

God is faithful to walk me through each day. I couldn't continue without Him. I guess we all go through seasons. Pray against the homesickness and for my back. I think my back is out. They can't do much here. My prayer is God will heal me.

The highlight of my summer is my little niece and nephew coming to visit at the end of June. My heart hurts over how I miss children, especially family. I've not seen a child in months. Blessings!

Journal

The homesickness set into depression. Last night, I was overcome with fear, worry, and doubt. I had a terrible dream about Mike. I cried for at least an hour straight and woke up this morning exhausted. When I told Mike in tears over the phone, he seemed to pull away. I don't want to make things worse for him; he's already having a difficult time. I prayed to the LORD to control my dreams, so why this scary dream about Mike?

When fear sets in, I feel like I can't move on. I'm at the end of my rope. I've prayed over our marriage all day. Why do I feel like there's something wrong? I hate that there's nothing I can do. Three hours a week with my husband isn't enough time. I feel like a burden to Mike. I hate telling people I'm not doing well. I don't want their pity or to upset them. No one handles it when Brandy isn't doing well.

Lord, take these feelings away. Forgive me of unbelief and worry. Only You can help me and know how I feel. No one understands, and I only add to their stress. I know You have a plan, but my future seems dark. Work in my favor and give me the strength to endure until the end.

June 10, 2008

Journal

Sam just left, and I don't feel as homesick. I'm struggling with my relationship with Mike. I feel like if I tell him my weaknesses, he'll fall under the pressure. He's not been to church because of my visits. He's not getting into the Word or even praying. He's weak, and I have to be an encouragement to him. I'm worried about him, and that's wrong. I need to keep praying. Lord, help me to trust You alone through this and draw Mike back to You.

I pray the same for all those that need to depend on You. Keep them near You, protect them, and bind Satan from their lives. Defeat my thoughts of doubt, worry, and unbelief with Your truth. I need Your power to strengthen me and overcome my feelings and emotions. Thank You for my precious sister today. I love her so much. My soul has so many cries, and I'm thankful You hear them all.

June 12, 2008

Journal

Happy 4th Anniversary. I can't see Mike on my anniversary, but I'm thankful we are together. Our marriage has taken a lot of beatings and has come out stronger. I pray for continued healing, protection, and growth.

My therapist talked about pardons today. She said few sex offenders get them and challenged me to make it a long-term goal. There's much change discussed on the laws for sex offenders. I'll have to register much longer than my current five years. It's possible it could be for life. Words like this spoken make my stomach drop. I feel a seal of doom placed on my heart. Lord, hear my cry and deliver me. When is it enough?

My back is getting worse. They took X-rays and can't find anything. The staff told me to file a grievance because the doctor hasn't seen me. I haven't been able to exercise or walk. It's uncomfortable even to sit.

There was a fire yesterday at Mike's plant, and was minutes away from exploding. Mike was on the roof above the machine that caught fire. Thank You, God, for protecting my husband. I don't know what I'd do if I lost him, especially on our anniversary.

June 14, 2008

The doctor called me in about my back. The first thing out of his mouth was, "You have a question?" I explained my back pain as I did on the form. He rudely commented there isn't anything on the X-ray. He asked what I'm asking him to do since he denied me pain medicine. I asked if I could see a chiropractor and he freaked out. I looked at him firmly and said, "It was a question." Staff was unhappy with how he treated me.

Cheyenne always sits with me, but today she didn't. She's been avoiding me. I feel I've been time-warped back into junior high. I think it started last week when Kelly found out she had received her parole. It's huge that she got it and will be transitioning out soon.

Kelly was desperate to find a song her father had written on his goodbye note. She was searching in some magazines and mumbled a few lyrics. I recognized it as Jeremy Camp's "Take You Back."[8] By God's grace, I had the CD in my room! I gave it to her. It was the last thing he wrote before taking his life. I know it meant the world to Kelly to hear that song.

When I spend time with Kelly, Cheyenne gets upset. I'm asking for direction and compassion to resolve this tension surrounding me. I want to do a Bible study with Cheyenne, but I am hesitant. Help her trust level. Give her a heart for others beyond herself and give her eyes to see her need for You. I don't want to be a hindrance to her.

June 16, 2008

I can't believe it was our first anniversary apart. You were so distraught when you walked into the room because our food order

---

[8] "Take You Back," *Restored*, (BEC Recordings; Jeremy Camp), 2004.

was wrong. I'm excited we can eat together and will eat anything from a restaurant. If I were in York, we'd be eating chips and a candy bar. I'm glad you liked the Noah's Ark latch hook and model car I made in hobby time. I can't get over how sad you looked.

It reminds me of Six Flags in college. I planned to tell you I wanted to be your girlfriend after months of you begging. The whole scene was painted in my mind. I'd take you on the two story carousel all lit up that evening. As we got in line, the worker said it had just broken down. I was devastated as I'd waited so long to announce this next step in our relationship. You'd said seeing me upset made the moment better because you saw how much it meant to me. I say the same thing to you.

I've been praying through today. I don't want to get homesick like I did last Sunday after you left. Nobody wants to play a game. I need a partner, and that's you. We got through another week, which is one less until I'm back with you. Getting back to you fuels me to keep going, especially on the hardest days. You're my motivation, and God is my strength. I love you, Michael Denham, with all my heart.

June 18, 2008

You said last year we have to put God in first place in our lives for our marriage to work. I feel like I've started leaning too much on you. There's nothing wrong with you making me feel happy, but I need to depend on God alone to get me through this. You can and do encourage me, but He alone gives me the strength I need.

I'm sorry I add to your pain. I try to be open and vulnerable with you, but I know there's a price with that. I'm sorry I allow my fears and worries to get to me. We'll make it through this. We have to claim victory now and not let Satan discourage us. God wants me to remain faithful.

I got through another TPR. They freak me out as I sit twelve against one. Dee asked when I'd want to go back to York if they released me. I said the fall because I'm eligible for Work Release then. I was supposed to receive my score, but not all the staff turned them in.

Later, my social worker accidentally congratulated me on receiving Level III. Dee said Dr. Mann has to tell me. He'll probably wait a while to tell me. I'm nervous as this is the final level.

June 28, 2008

Journal

I walked into Visiting, where Mike and my in-laws already were. It was Mike's parents, both his sisters and their husbands, his two-year-old niece, and his four-year-old nephew. I haven't seen them in a year. Mike busied himself with food prep.

After hugs and hellos, we sat to eat. My nephew jumped into my lap. I miss children with every fiber of my being. I haven't seen a child in a year, let alone those whom love their Aunt Brandy. I felt this sickness wash over me as the staff watched my every move. I felt like they were waiting for something awful to happen. I hate feeling like I'm under a microscope, and like everyone secretly doubts me.

Despite my thoughts, the staff was kind. I'm very grateful they voted I could have a visit from my small niece and nephew. It's rare for someone here to receive such a visit, especially from in-laws.

After lunch, the adults played *Phase 10*. I didn't get much time to talk to Mike's mom. I greatly appreciate her support and would've struggled so much more without her. We took lots of pictures and soon our time was over. Cheryl started crying really hard, which set off one of Mike's sisters. Like dominos, we all fell under the weight of this moment. I demanded my stupid tears to stay put, but I couldn't fight their fall.

We agreed time went too quickly; it'd be too long until we see each other, and that life just isn't fair. We embraced, and then I watched each of them round the corner, leaving this awful place. I stopped the pressure to resist, letting the tears flow and give way to the emotions burning inside my body. There I remained, wishing to round the corner behind them and go home with my family.

Thank You, God, for being near when I feel so far from everyone. I'm thankful You got me through that. I'm in prison, a treatment center, locked up behind a scary brick building with the most dangerous sex offenders in the state. What can my family say to someone like me? No one can save me. Mike's family is amazing. They gave me candy, phone cards, pajamas, and magazines. Thank You for my in-laws and that You got me through this difficult but uplifting day. But please, Lord, get me home soon.

June 30, 2008

It was my turn to have the TV. *Nanny McPhee* was on when Ben came in. He said the movie wasn't age appropriate and asked if I had any attractions or arousals. The oldest child in the movie is ten. In my disgust, I got up to leave. His motivation was to watch *Family Guy*. He barked at me to give him the remote. I said, "What do you say?" He swore at me to give him the remote. He and Kelly laughed as they started watching their show. Later, Ben stood in my window, waving and smiling as if everything was fine.

I read my Bible and studies. My takeaway was from *Corrie Ten Boom*.[9] She and her sister were in a concentration camp and put into a cell infested with bugs, fleas and lice. Corries's sister said they needed

---

[9] Carole C. Carlson, *Corrie Ten Boom: Her Life, Her Faith* (Alresford: Christian Literature Crusade, 1983).

to be thankful. Corrie said, "Even for the fleas and lice?" Corrie couldn't be thankful like her sister and felt ashamed. She found out later it was because of those pests that guards wouldn't go into their cell to beat and rape them. Corrie and her sister spread the Gospel without being punished. I need to be thankful I'm here with these pests. Who knows what I'm dodging at York?

God gives us what we need when we need it. When Corrie was a girl, she told her dad, "I'll never be able to witness and suffer for Jesus."

He said, "Corrie, when Daddy buys you a train ticket, does he give it to you three weeks before or right before you go?"

She said, "Right before I go."

He replied, "The same is true of God. He'll give you what you need when you need it, never before."

If someone would've told me I'd be sentenced to four to eight years, go to Segregation, a mental institution, be a sex offender, and never teach children again, I would've given up the ghost. There's no way I could've handled it. I barely handle it now.

God gives strength, courage, love, and protection when we need it. His grace is sufficient. I can't think of a day when I couldn't say so. We will make it through this. We'll have bumps ahead, but we can look back to this mountain and say, "God was faithful yesterday, so He'll be faithful today."

I thoroughly enjoyed your laughing while visiting. It was music to my ears and air to my lungs. I don't remember why you were laughing, but it was real. It thrilled my heart to experience your pure happiness. It'd been so long, and I didn't want it to stop. I wish I could trap it into a little bottle and open it up whenever I needed it.

Tonight was the most fun I've had in a long time. When you shine like that, my heart can't help but soar. I miss you so incredibly much and now the floodgates of tears have opened. I love you. You are my rock.

July 1, 2008

One year ago today, Grandpa passed away. Memories flooded of times being with him, working on his rentals, organizing his shop, going to festivals, finding my first car, and so many lunches after church. I still hear his voice singing, "Brandy, you're a fine girl..."[10]

I called to check in on Grandma. She said Grandpa always said, "You can't do anything about the past, so just move forward." If only my forward didn't look so tainted. I'll hold Grandpa in my heart forever. I'm thankful he didn't give up on me when the church did. Even at my worst, he loved me well.

My friend visited and brought me a hymnal. It's been a while since I've seen a hymnal. It's bittersweet thinking of singing those hymns in my childhood church, where I'm no longer welcome or allowed. God, please heal my broken heart.

July 13, 2008

Journal

Sundays hit hard. I'm overwhelmed with pain from the past. I keep having nightmares. I desperately want to repair my marriage. One short, chaotic summer wasn't long enough to put back the pieces.

I want to run so hard I can't breathe and feel my heart explode with life. Instead, I sit in a chair, trying to entertain myself. Sometimes I wonder if I'll make it through. One minute, I'm okay, and the next, I'm scraping myself off the ground.

---

[10] "Brandy (You're a Fine Girl)," *Looking Glass,* (Epic Records; Looking Glass), 1972.

I want to leave Nebraska and start over when I get out. I'll play Rascal Flatts, "I'm Movin' On"[11] as we leave. I know I screwed up big time, but I've done everything I can. I know God is in control and has a purpose. Please tell my heart, soul, and future that. It's so scary.

I pour my life into others, but I feel empty. Fill me with Your love. Help me to feel it. Empty me of myself. You alone are my strength, power, and desire. Don't leave me. I don't have words, but You know my bleeding heart. Heal it, God. Pour out Your healing onto my gaping wounds. Forget my pain, sin, shame, and guilt. Help me live in You and You in me. Draw me close and take over.

The homesickness and depression cloud rained over my bed. I felt myself drowning under its weight. I looked out my small window and saw exploding fireworks in the distance. It's almost Independence Day, followed by my birthday.

I can't do another holiday and birthday in prison. I love summer with my entire being. I love the beach, swimming, the hot sun, and just being outside. At the sight of the colors lighting up the night sky, my emotions released with equal exploding power. I felt myself spiraling down into the pit of depression. I need help.

---

[11] "I'm Movin' On," *Rascal Flatts* (Lyric Street Records; Rascal Flatts), 2001.

CHAPTER 13

The Love Chapter

I climbed into bed and recited the verse I've quoted every night since being incarcerated. Tonight, the verse settled on a whole new level. Psalm 57:1, "Be merciful unto me, O God, be merciful unto me: for my soul trusted in thee: yeah, in the shadow of thy wings will I make my refuge until all these calamities be over past." That verse makes me feel safe and secure under the wing of God.

I lay under my feather comforter and cuddled in closer. As I prayed, I felt the love of God washing over me. A strong warm surge flowed over my body as the events of this past year came to mind.

God brought to remembrance one of my weakest moments last summer when I was in Vegas. I'd lost my home, marriage, reputation, and career. I was afraid of what legal ramifications lay ahead. I'd hit rock bottom. I cried to God and heard Him clearly say, "Be still and know that I am God."

The Lord has gotten me through this year, even when I had no hope in anyone or anything. As He brought to mind all these places I've traveled, my heart grew thankful that God never left me. All I wanted was Jesus. I could feel His arms around me and actually felt God's love. I've never felt anything like it before.

I cried into my pillow for an hour with such a desire to know God more. He allowed me to feel His love. The words, "To know the love of God," kept repeating in my mind. There was such great peace deep inside, and I felt I was in the very presence of the King. It didn't matter that I was locked up. I felt God take me somewhere else, where nothing mattered.

Ephesians 3:19, "And to know the love of Christ, which passeth knowledge, that ye might be filled with all the fulness of God." That's exactly how I felt. The worry, homesickness, and fear were gone, and only the fullness of God remained.

July 14, 2008

I'll have to register as a sex offender the day after my birthday. I felt this weird shift. It's as if serving time, living in a mental institution, never teaching again, and enduring all this pain isn't enough. I'll have to go through so much more when I get out.

I walked outside and fought back tears. I haven't cried in front of anyone, but inside, I feel like I'm drowning. When I get like this, it's difficult to see God clearly, and spending time with Him isn't what it ought to be. It feels like He's still mad at me, and being with Him feels like a duty rather than a desire.

I'm struggling that I can't see or hug you whenever I want. I hope we appreciate and enjoy each other more after this. I've always struggled with slowing down enough to enjoy life. I don't want my life to fly by and ask, "Where did my life go?" I want to treasure every moment of my freedom and live life to the fullest.

I've been sighing my way through this day and didn't realize it. One of my peers pointed it out. I find comfort when you talk of the future we'll have together. My fears and worries seem smaller with you by my side through the registering process and the rest of the trenches we'll trudge through. I want to move past this and be left alone. I long for no spying, prying, questions, testings, assessments, and dissecting for all to see.

July 17, 2008

Journal

Wow, it's my birthday, and I'm in prison, in an institution at that. Last night I was given a great gift from God. He allowed me to regain my focus on Him where it belongs. I looked at my present circumstances and future, and I'd begun to sink. I was pretty depressed this past week. I lost hope and shut down.

After a night of crying out to God, I felt His presence once again. I cannot do this alone. I'm only this far because of God. He promises to forgive and help us when we call out to Him. Satan's been attacking relentlessly. I suppose that should mean something. If I really were a worthless cause, Satan wouldn't want anything to do with me. I still shrink about my future. I need to trust God no matter how dark the future and present may be.

I received several birthday cards yesterday. Staff joked they needed to hire another member to watch me open mail. Mike sang to me and said he wanted to get my name tattooed on him for my birthday. As corny as that sounds, it made me feel pretty special. I look forward to our visit together later this week. The day is over, along with my birthday for another year. I pray I'm home for my next one.

July 20, 2008

You just left and my heart longs for you already. We covered some pretty heavy discussion that'll be helpful once I get home. We talked about where I'd like to move after this part of my life is over. It'll be difficult to move from home, but if my restrictions cut me down to a little lifeless nub, I'd rather not be home. It's too painful and I want to leave.

Thank you for the ring you bought me. I'm excited for it to be cleared so I can wear it. It'll be nice to have that connection again. I miss my wedding ring so much. I'm thankful our love has grown stronger in this long and dark season. A fire burning deep inside drives me to work hard to get home to you. Please don't ever give up on me. I may be down for a moment, but I'll get back up and press forward. I'm only strong in God's power.

Paul could rejoice in a dungeon because he had settled the issue of why he was living. He was not living to please himself or to get his needs fulfilled. He had one burning passion: to live for the glory and pleasure of God. All that mattered to him was knowing Christ and making Him known to others.

"True joy is not the absence of pain, but the presence of the LORD Jesus in the midst of the pain" (Nancy L. DeMoss).

July 22, 2008

Journal

I've been discouraged by our groups as therapists talk to us as a whole. It's as if we are exactly the same person cut from the same cloth. We're all labeled and in the same box.

I've been plagued with racing thoughts since a visit from a family member of Charles. It was good to see her, but she started talking about Charles, Jackie, their baby, and their vacation. It cut me to the core. After she left, I felt sick and empty. Fighting my feelings, I roamed aimlessly for hours and finally went to my room. I curled up in a ball in the corner of my bed and sobbed uncontrollably.

I felt so alone and worthless. Then I was mad at myself for not being healed and able to hear her share about their amazing lives. They've hurt me so deeply. The last thing I wanted to hear was their wonderful lives, but then I felt bad. I want them to be happy, but I want them to stay away.

I've been cut off and isolated. I haven't been home in over a year. I cried myself to sleep but awoke soaking wet in sweat. I awoke in a bad mood that continued all day. I couldn't help but spill it over the phone to Mike. I don't want him to worry about me, but I seriously felt like I'd rather die. I'm deeply depressed. I felt the world on my chest and couldn't breathe. The pressure was so heavy that my heart couldn't beat. This has been one of the worst days since I've been here.

My peers could sense something was going on. Cheyenne kept saying I'd be out of here soon. When we were outside, I wanted to break out and run. I wanted to scream at the top of my lungs, but I have to hold it all in. After I walked past everyone sitting on the benches, I'd cry out to God. I worked out my emotions almost to the breaking point, but I didn't have much time. I'd circle back around only thirty seconds later, so I'd suck it up in front of everyone. I repeated this process for about forty minutes. I thought I was going to pass out.

Kelly said when I'm not in the day hall, they always call for me to come back in. I think they find comfort in having me around, and I scared them today. I don't want them to feel scared just because I am.

The newest woman, Tess, asked me if she'd done something to offend me. I explained I was down about the constant rehashing of details in group without any assignments or areas to improve on. I shared I feel like I'm worthless and beat myself up over again. What's the use of moving forward if this is all I'll ever amount to?

She said I was unlike any of the stereotypical SOs we talk about and that I'm here for a reason. I argued, saying I don't feel like I'm accomplishing anything. With tears in her eyes, she said that I truly cared about her and she was grateful for me. She said that I help her and the others more than all the therapists combined. She cried and said my presence alone helped her. She seemed convinced, but it didn't seem to penetrate my depressed heart.

I called Mike's mom afterward. I had a feeling Mike called her already and told her how I was doing. She listened and began her speech on changing my attitude. She said she couldn't understand my pain, but God was using me tremendously in the lives of the women at York. Women wrote her about how they wouldn't have kept their faith or survived prison without me.

Then she said she was proud of me. That's what impacted me most. She's seen me grow tremendously this past year. This growth wasn't achievable without suffering and hardship.

I felt my fierce cries were answered. Again, I cried, but this time I felt washed with joy. I needed to refocus to help those around me and not worry about my future. My future is secure with Christ, and He'll give me what I need when I need it. God, I beg You to keep my eyes, mind, heart, body, and spirit on You alone. I cannot do this alone. I need You; please let me feel Your love.

CHAPTER 14

Follow Through

July 24, 2008

Journal

In RP, we discussed a crime in the media about a man who assaulted an eight-year-old. The details made me physically sick. Rita explained the crime we committed is the same exact thing. I feel defeated. I know my identity and worth aren't found in society and laws. Creator God tells me who I am, but I'm struggling. God, pick me up and plant my feet on You, my solid ground. Help me overcome opposition, even if my opposition was once my cheering section. I don't need people; I need Jesus.

July 25, 2008

Our snacks disappeared from the dayroom storage. Rita addressed it in group, which was a nightmare. Somehow she related it to our

143

sexual assault cycle, because everything in life relates to our sexual assault cycle.

She wanted each of us to share who we thought did it. I didn't blame anyone because I don't know. The others voiced their thoughts, and it became a screaming bloodbath. Cheyenne was attacked most and became angry and defensive. I'm not sure what this exercise was supposed to accomplish. We're all being punished with food suspension until further notice.

Cheyenne isn't talking to anyone, including me. She won't even look at me. She said she doesn't trust anyone and wants to go back to York.

July 31, 2008

Journal

We continued talking about the snack thief in our one-on-ones. We beat a dead horse, and our relationships are suffering. My attitude has been horrible. I walked around outside, upset that I was questioning God's purpose for me here. The circumstances were unfair, but I needed to surrender and obey.

In my internal struggle, I heard God whisper to ask Cheyenne to do a Bible study. Seriously? She won't sit with me, talk to me, or look at me. I'd just surrendered to obey God no matter what He asks of me, so here it goes. God gave me the words because I had no idea how to approach her. She said, "Yes." I was shocked and nervous, but I felt we needed to start today.

We did Tara's Bible study, *Resting in His Reality*.[12] I explained the plan of salvation to her and asked if she was ready to ask Jesus into

---

[12] Tara Rye, *Resting In His Reality*, 2007.

her life. She nodded, so we prayed together, and she asked Christ into her heart. She revealed she's in the exact place she needed to be. If this is what God put into her life, she'd trust Him to lead.

She was no longer angry at God that her baby had passed away. God had a plan. I've never seen her smile like that. It's a smile I'll never forget because she had absolute joy. It was a visible transformation that I was blessed to encounter. God at work. We are going to do a study every day. Help me as I disciple this new believer. Give me the words her growing heart needs to hear and receive.

I was ready to quit today, and You worked a miracle through me, despite me. You answered many prayers. Kelly was also in the room during much of our discussion. Work in that too. Let Cheyenne's light continue shining and not burn out. Allow her life to change many others.

Forgive me of my doubt, fear, unbelief, self-pity, and every other sin that clouded my view of seeing who You are. I'm speechless and in awe. Thank You for being such an awesome God. There's no greater joy than to see one come to You. Thank You for using me today.

I saw Dr. Mann after. God gave me peace and words to speak. He asked me about receiving Level III and my parole and jam date. I added the Work Release eligibility date. He seemed supportive of my desire and said I can return anytime after completion. He brought up the stealing of snacks situation and asked why I wasn't accused by others. I responded that I didn't know, for I'm not better than anyone else. It was quick, and I was out the door.

Today's been a blessing, and I don't want to lose the wonder of it. Let me see more of You through this. Restore the joy of my salvation and give me the strength to get through this program. I praise Your name and give You glory for the great things You have done! Thank You, Lord.

August 3, 2008

Cheyenne and I did a study on the wise man who built his house on the rock. It described the meaning of the song, "This Little Light of Mine." I watched her eyes open to the truth as she shared she sang it on the reservation during VBS as a child. Watching this revelation unfold and bearing witness to how it impacted her was like unwrapping a precious gift. The songs finally made sense, and she understood the words behind the songs. It was incredible.

There are rumors about what Dr. Mann said about my return. Some of the staff don't think I've completed all levels. I feel like some are upset with me, including Ben. They've been taking some privileges away, like they're trying to test me. Now my peers are upset and blame me for it. It's difficult for them. Kelly's been here for two years. It only took me seven months. The other two are still at Level I.

For the Website

Thanks for praying for my meetings. I expressed my desire to return to York after completion of this program in hopes of going to Work Release. This is what we've been praying for, but seems silly to be excited about going back to prison.

I have no idea how long I'll be there before I go to Work Release. I feel overwhelmed leaving my environment again, especially with so many uncertainties. However, this is my next step in getting home.

I'll be in D&E when I go back. I've never been there because I went to Segregation the first time. While in D&E, I'll have limited ways of communicating and visiting. It sounds like I'll be leaving sometime after Labor Day. Please keep your lifeline letters flowing. Thank you for your faithfulness to us. Love you all!

August 5, 2008

Journal

I had my one-on-one with Ben. He prods like an old schemer with off-the-wall questions he labels "therapy." He's not a therapist, but rather a glorified babysitter with horrible morals and values. He spreads whatever I share in confidence after twisting it out of context. He sneers as he lies and generates turmoil. I struggle to have a heart for him, knowing he's lost. He never congratulated me on getting to Level III. Instead, he congratulated Kelly on her amazing leadership skills.

Kelly was able to go home for a few hours since she's transitioning out. She came back in a good mood and we had a good conversation. I'm happy for her, but my heart aches. I want to go home. Why can't I return? You can do anything. What's wrong with me? I feel the darkness will swallow me whole. No one understands what I have to walk through or can even try to relate. I know You see me. Please help me.

August 25, 2008

I met with Dr. Mann. He said I could go back as soon as I submit a letter of request. I asked how long it would take to leave after I submitted the request. He said a day, but later a therapist said it'd take a while. I get different answers from everyone.

I could stay and transition out like Kelly, but I'd wait a whole year until I'm eligible for parole. I don't want to return to prison, but it's the only way I get to Work Release. There, I'll get an overnight home and far more privileges than here.

A couple of staff members said going back isn't wise. I wish I had encouragement for the next step. Instead, it's going over the worst, being stuck in the past, and rehashing everything.

I'm afraid I'll be stuck at York on a waiting list. Will I get harassed and threatened like before? The staff continues asking questions, so I keep fearing the worst. There are comforts here I don't have at York. It's also half the drive for everyone.

I always circle back to the fact God opened this door. I have to go back to the pit to come out the other side. I need to trust God and have faith despite fears of the unknown. Please help me follow through.

August 26, 2008

Journal

My sister just left. She heads back to college tomorrow. She'll visit during her next break, but I don't know where I'll be. It feels like someone has taken a piece of me away. Draw her close, protect her, and may she never make the same mistakes I did. It comforts me, knowing You love her more than I do.

I met with Dee to discuss my TPR results. Rumors fly because no one has ever completed treatment this quickly. The confusion takes away the excitement I want to feel from completing my program. I don't want to take the long road back through prison. I feel like I'm getting the "Go straight to jail" card all over again, rather than collecting anything positive for working hard. It's all stripped away.

September 2, 2008

Journal

I stare at my few things all packed up. I submitted my request to return to York upon completion of my program. It's such a big deal, yet Dr. Mann said it didn't matter who I turned it in to.

Dee said Dr. Mann wouldn't return for several days and has to sign my discharge. The head psychiatrist said Dr. Mann would be here in ten minutes. Ten minutes turned into two hours. Dr. Mann said I'd be gone within the day and to pack up. After I told the therapist, she laughed and said not to expect that timeframe. I asked her if there was a general frame I could expect. She said we would talk tomorrow.

So here I lay, staring at my stuff. I took my pictures off the wall. I cried myself to sleep last night, thinking of being in prison today. I'll go through this entire process all over again.

I called Mike and shared my emotions. He replied, "I told you not to pack!" I want to tell him this isn't fair. He can go where he wants, when he wants, and do whatever he wants. I've had enough. I'm turning bitter. God help me! Here lies another test. When is it enough?

Everyone keeps saying I'll get stuck at York. I'm growing tired of all the discouragement. Many say, "Maybe there's someone that needs your help." There are hurting people everywhere that need help. God doesn't need me.

I expect the worst to happen because I've been conditioned to it. My length of sentence, Segregation, prison, and mental institution. I rejoice in what God has walked me through, but in the same breath, I'm done. My path seems dark. I'll travel through Work Release (hopefully) and then parole back into a community where I've been cut off. I'll have to register for all to see.

I desire to be a present wife and become a mother. Isn't my family supposed to be first? I've done everything asked. I'll have to live forever with this label branded on my heart. I'll continue with parole beyond my sentence. My mind spins, and I'm physically sick. I lay down yet continue writing.

I want to tell Mike everything, but I'll bring him down. He's visiting his parents while I'm stuck in limbo. Forgive me for my horrible attitude and impatience. I know You are working when I cannot see You. I'm thankful that even when I'm a royal pain and don't deserve anything, You declare me worthy because of who You are. Thank You for Your mercy and grace that I don't deserve.

Please remember I'm a mere human and very weak. I'm only strong when I stand with You. Strong or not, I want to go home. What I wouldn't do to feel freedom, hang out with Mike, play with my dogs, take a bath with bubbles, play in the ocean after walking on the shore, or walk to the park. It's been so long. Please get me home soon. Forgive me for all I've done, and work this together for good. Amen.

September 5, 2008

Journal

I'm anxious to leave. I finally saw a sliver of light through a cracked open door. The light revealed the next step, but that light has grown dark. I'm on the destination home, but the door is shut. My expectations shrink, and everything feels like it's falling apart.

My head tells me it's part of God's plan and will work out for His glory, but my heart screams, "I want to go home!" Hope turns dark, and I doubt I'll ever make it. Friends try to assure me that I'll be fine. They have no idea what I'll enter in prison. God, please help me. I know I did wrong, but I've paid dearly and will continue paying my entire life. Why can't I go home?

I should be praying for others and not wallowing in self-pity. Forgive me, but right now my way seems dark and unsure. I can't see the way and my tears run freely. I can't do this. I'm currently in a mental institution wanting to go back to prison. There's no way out. I'm trapped and unable to breathe. When, God?

September 6, 2008

Journal

I finally unpacked my clothes. I'm thankful for my aunt coming today. Tonya's my only aunt that visits. She's brought me the new flavor of Mountain Dew, which is my jam. It's been sweet to develop our relationship. Our visit was interpreted by Dee. Dr. Mann wanted me to resubmit one sentence stating I wanted to return to York. It was time for Tonya to leave, and she cried like I've never seen her cry before. It made me feel special and loved. It was difficult, but we said our goodbyes.

Dr. Mann paid us a surprise visit. He told me I was going back to prison on Monday. I'm leaving the day after tomorrow. I must prepare internally and externally. It would be so much easier if I knew how long I'd get hung up at York. God, please calm my heart and all my fears.

September 7, 2008

Journal

This is my last night at LRC. Mike was frustrated with me on the phone. He said he doesn't know who he's talking to lately. One minute I'm doing well and the next I'm depressed. What does he expect? It's difficult to convey exactly what I'm thinking and feeling over the phone.

I honestly don't know how I'm feeling. I'm all over the place. I don't want to bug him while he's on vacation with his family. It seems if I share, he can't take it. It's difficult for him to hear me going through this. I want to be able to share my thoughts and feelings. I'm tired of holding them back in fear of upsetting him.

I don't know how to pray. When I think of all that lies before me, the tears escape. You know what I've walked through already and what lies ahead. Please give me the strength to say goodbyes and enter York tomorrow. I'm struggling with keeping it together. It affects the women I've been with for the past seven months as well as staff. Ben said I need to pack up all the happiness with me because I give this place a bad rap.

I know this is my next step, so God, give me the strength to do it. Give me peace. I'm scared. I shouldn't be, but I am. It feels like my outcome is always the opposite of what I want. Again, I know this is Your plan, and Your way is perfect. I'm glad You go with me, and I'm not alone. Surround me with Your presence, guide me, and take me far away from what I'm walking through. Right now, things are so quiet, deathly quiet, but quiet. That all goes away tomorrow. I'll miss the quiet. Help me, Lord. In Jesus' name. AMEN.

CHAPTER 15

Diagnostic and Evaluation

September 9, 2008

I made it to York. Sorry I couldn't call and let you know. The lieutenant said I couldn't call because I'm a transfer. I arrived in handcuffs and was welcomed by a strip search. I'll have to get used to that again. I saw Becky, as she works Intake. She's the one I prayed with before I left. She was scared I was sent back. Everyone will think the same. Women don't go back to prison after completing programming. I'm a prison unicorn.

As I walked to D&E, women were headed to lunch. They stopped and started whispering while glaring at me. I'm so not ready to be back here. I went straight into my cell with two women. Anna is Russian, in her mid-thirties. Joanna is my age and a Christian. I've waited forever to talk to another believer. It's awesome, except she leaves Thursday for Work Release. Both of them leave, so I'll be alone until new women arrive.

We're locked in our cells at different times throughout the day. We're designated activity time, outside time, and learning rules by watching outdated prison videos. No one knows if my visiting forms are active, so I'm sending new ones. I'll buy phone time soon as I can. Hopefully, my phone sheet will get back soon. This letter took me two hours to write, as Anna talks nonstop.

Women eligible for Work Release are placed on a waiting list. Those with shorter sentences leave first. Work Release has limited space, so the waiting list is long. New inmates with shorter sentences get priority over women with longer sentences that have waited on the list. I'll have to wait. Women who have never set foot on the yard head to Work Release before me. I've been locked up for a whole year, and they barely arrive and leave.

I saw Daisy and Nicole as I walked to Medical, but they didn't see me. I wanted to shout, but we can't communicate with those on the yard. At least I'm not chained up this time around. I praise God for that.

Someone asked if I'd buy them Canteen and another hit on me. I shut it down. The showers are basically open to anyone looking in that direction. Whoever you shower next to can see you. The prison is just asking for issues to happen.

September 10, 2008

I didn't sleep. D&E has uncomfortable boat-like beds. I lay under the vent that blows directly on me with a bright light shining in my eyes. Anna's nice, but loud and easily angered. She says I calm her and begs me to keep talking.

I enjoy Joanna. It's been a while since I've spent time around another believer. This is our last night before she leaves. We've shared stories, and I feel a connection with her.

Terry's still here. I heard she was transferred to another institution, but she's here. I'm now really dreading the yard. Why can't I get sent out of here instead? I've completed the most difficult treatment program in the entire institution faster than anyone. Shouldn't that count for something? I've done my part. SAU counselors don't want women back on the yard after treatment. Why am I different? Why is my path always the most difficult?

Everyone stops, stares, and whispers every time I go to Medical. They think I failed and was sent back. I don't want to go back to the most violent hall in prison. Tomorrow I'll be alone here. Everyone in D&E is headed to Work Release or the yard. I came separately and had to wait for the next batch of women.

September 12, 2008

I've only been back three days, but it feels like an eternity. Time crawls by with nothing to do and not being able to talk to or see you. I got my first letter from your mom, which I desperately needed. I asked a guard when I would get visits. He didn't know because I'm not considered orientation, and he doesn't know my classification. I'm always the odd woman out. I should get a visit tomorrow, but I haven't received my forms, and the case manager is out all weekend.

The guard that stripped me down for Medical said, "What's going on? Why are you back?" She said I'm the talk of the yard and that I should kite someone because it's pretty screwed up that I came back here.

While waiting for Medical, I saw Daisy. She jumped out of her skin when she recognized me. She waved the beloved half-sheet of paper in her hand as she yelled that she was headed to Work Release.

We came to prison at the same time and have the same sentence. Oh, I hope by some miracle that I will go with her.

I wish I had someone to talk to. I used to process my thoughts with an entire treatment staff. It's an adjustment going from talking myself blue in the face to being cut off. I don't trust any of these women. Whenever I kindly talk, they start their questions about why I'm here.

My phone sheet was messed up. They entered the number wrong. At least I figured out why I couldn't call anyone. I'll try tomorrow. I would've walked outside in the rain, but used my only hour outside my cell to figure out what was wrong with my phone sheet.

I've received the approval for visitors! I'm so excited you can come tomorrow. Hopefully, I'll get my phone sheet back, so I can let someone know about the visit. I can't wait to see you. I'll look horrible, as I wasn't allowed to keep anything I had. I've been washing my hair with a bar of soap.

I got ahold of your mom, and she'll tell you. Though it was raining, we were allowed outside. It felt good to walk in the rain. Why've I not enjoyed walking around in the rain before? I don't care about the same things in prison. It felt refreshing and just what my desperate soul needed.

After my walk, I went to my cell. I'm not my normal social self in D&E. It feels unsafe. Of course, it's unsafe, I'm in prison, but I'm used to prison. These women aren't safe for me to share with, or at least not now. They're caught up in little cliques and talk about pretty grotesque stuff. I'm desperate for encouraging conversation.

September 13, 2008

I wait to hear my name being called to Visiting. I seriously look terrible. My face is breaking out. My shower time is at the same time as Visiting, so I don't get a shower. I'm not allowed contacts here, so it's my glasses again. Hopefully, you'll recognize me, and you can calm this girl down. There's my name.

I'm so glad I saw you, even though it was cut short. I felt all I talked about was my fears about hitting the yard. My worry can't change anything. I just feel like I'm taking a step back. I've done my time here. I want to enjoy the privileges of Work Release. I'm afraid if I hit the yard, they'll forget about me. Despite what I want, I know (through very thick clouds) God is for me. I haven't been at peace because I haven't been trusting.

A woman came with a guitar for our church service. We sang familiar praise songs together; then, she read her message off a sheet of paper. She said we shouldn't worry, but trust God. I'll forever be learning this lesson.

September 14, 2008

Two minors in the cell next door always get seated at my table at mealtime. They walk around like they own the place. If you'll recall, guards supposed I went to Segregation because there were minors in D&E, and because of my charge, I wasn't allowed near them. Cheyenne said she went to D&E, and there was a minor with her. I don't think I'll ever know the reason they put me into Segregation.

I finally met with my caseworker. I have enough points for Work Release, but I don't qualify until the 26th. That day, I'll get put on the list and wait for an opening. The parole board approves ten spots at a time, so it's difficult to know when the next bus will come. It's not the news I wanted to hear, but at least I know.

I know God will go with me and protect me, but I'm still scared. Why did I get my hopes up that I could go straight to Work Release? Why am I so weak? I just want to climb into a hole and hide until my time is up. Do you have any idea how many people maul me with questions? I can do this with God's help, but I absolutely don't want to. Why is every step heart-wrenching, treacherous, humiliating, unknown, and full of shifting shadows? I just wish something would be easy for once.

I just got off the phone with you. Your response to me hitting the yard is, "You've got this; it's no big deal." I guess you'd need to be in prison to understand where I'm coming from. You should see the other women that are about to hit the yard. They're freaking out with fear and stress, including those that have been here before and know what to expect. I feel shut down when I try to explain myself to you. You either respond with, "It's not a big deal," or don't respond at all.

I have only fifteen minutes a day to talk to someone, and that someone is you. I feel belittled because of how scared I am. I'm not perfect, strong, or anything else. I'm lonely, afraid, weak, and want to go home in a very overwhelming way. I'm tired of my stupid life. I feel like a loser when I express my feelings. Apparently, I am one since I'm still in prison.

You make it seem like this is a cakewalk, and it honestly ticks me off. Fifteen minutes of silence or being brushed off is unbelievable. I'm obviously upset. I don't even know when they'll make me go to the yard. I absolutely hate going through all this again.

Now I feel guilty that I'm upset with you. You must feel helpless and don't know what to say. I only get a sliver of time, and I feel worse than before. I hoped my attitude would've changed. Now, I feel like I've disappointed you. I'm at rock bottom all over again. The tears flow and won't stop. I want to be brave and strong, but I can't even lift my head. I just wish you could experience where I'm at, so you could understand. I'm sorry. I love you.

September 15, 2008

I couldn't call you because we had no free time due to haircuts. I'll have to wait until tomorrow. Two women arrived that were sent back from Work Release. One said she had a bad UA, but was retested and cleared. The other said she came back from work late. They both said it's easy to get sent back.

My caseworker classified me well over the points needed for Work Release, but I must wait until the 26th to qualify. Then she said to pack up because I was hitting the yard. It's not a typical day they send out women, so I was the only one.

CHAPTER 16

I'm Back

I hauled my two giant bags full of state-issued clothes and bedding. I about passed out. North Hall is on the other side of the prison. I could barely pick the bags up, let alone carry them.

I have one cellmate named Amy. She seems laid back, which is a miracle. Daisy was excited to see me. Everyone has told me how excited Daisy was that I was back. I'm glad she's here, but she leaves soon. I really want to leave with her. I don't get classified until later this week, so I have no job until then.

Daisy's across the hall, with Terry, of all people. Terry still hates me with a passion. She told Daisy she'd respect her even though she's friends with me. Terry's a temporary cellmate as her cell has mold in it. Hopefully, she goes back soon. I don't want to be in the same wing again, let alone across from her.

Daisy's asking her boss to hire me at Canteen. It's a fun job without all the drama. I love teaching, but I'm stressed about going back to school. Terry's still trying to get her GED, and the school's chaotic.

September 16, 2008

I'm glad I was able to talk to you this morning. I hate having a time limit again. Mrs. R found out I was back and paged me immediately to school. She was so excited to see me. She begged me to come back. Sigh, it's just so stressful. I hope I get a say where I go, but that's not how it works around here. The school is desperate for skilled TAs. I know I'll have to tough it out.

I started a Bible study in our hall. We shared our stories today. I connected with a woman named Shelly. She feels she already knows me as everyone has told her about me, especially the Peters. Shelly's beautiful, has several children, and has a long sentence. I was completely shocked by her sad story.

Amy, my cellmate, asked why I'm in prison. I don't feel threatened by her, and she's been very kind. She had already heard most of what I told her. She said my charge isn't who I am. She's an answer to prayer.

Thank you for writing. I know you're busy, but your words impact me the most. I look forward to seeing you this weekend. I start back at school tomorrow. It's definitely not the job I want, but I'm thankful for the blessings God has given.

September 17, 2008

I'm thankful time flies at school, but it's the most stressful job in prison. All the TAs have job changes submitted. The school is moving to another building to give us more space. The TAs have to move everything.

A woman from my Bible study wants to eat lunch together, but if I eat with her, Daisy won't join. Daisy can't associate with the woman because Terry's after her. I hate that I have to pick between them. I feel time-warped back to junior high, just with felons.

I'm so exhausted. I forgot how draining teaching is. I haven't worked for seven months. We start moving the school tomorrow. I'll be wiped out for sure.

September 19, 2008

I'm thankful I had a full conversation with you today in Visiting. My dad's coming tonight. I'm thankful to see him as well as eat vending machine snacks. We have something gross for dinner.

I saw my caseworker today and was classified. I qualify for Work Release, and they'll submit my paperwork. It goes through a long process of prison, parole board, LRC, and back here. That whole process takes four to six weeks, and then I get put on the waiting list. I need to stay out of trouble and wait.

I told my caseworker I was called into the school when I hit the yard and have been working since. She said she'd look into it. When I got back to school, Mrs. R had already talked to my caseworker. Mrs. R was asked if she wanted me, even though I wouldn't be staying long-term. Mrs. R said, "Even if it were one day, I'd take her." It's nice to feel needed, but I was hoping for a different job. The school gets priority over everything.

The new school is in the old D&E building. They unplugged the pop machine, but never took the pop out. Exploded cans are everywhere. Nothing's been there in three years. It's just one big room, so we'll be all together.

It took forever to get called to Visiting to see my dad. The poor guy hates to wait. *Welcome to my life, Dad.* I'm very thankful he brought lots of change. It reminded me of when we used to go to the Mini Mart, and he said we could pick one thing. It was never just one thing. I swear we kept that Mini-Mart running.

September 22, 2008

When I awoke, I was so sore that I could barely move. My body needs to adjust to walking like this again. We began packing and moving the school right away. Several TAs are loud, obnoxious, and bossy. They believe their ideas are best and let everyone know it. I felt tested the entire day. We worked through lockdown until dinner. I really have no desire to do this job, but I'm trying.

Thank God, I got approval in time for Bible study tonight. Al and Nadine were just as excited to see me as I was to see them. I sat with Shelly. I haven't met anyone like her and Joanna before.

September 23, 2008

Today was another long day of moving tons of boxes up four flights of stairs. After dinner, I walked with Shelly. She showed me pictures of her children. It's heartbreaking to think about how the twins she was pregnant with in county will be adults when she gets out. They'll hardly know their mother. Her husband hasn't brought them to see her. Hearing her heartache reminds me of my own. I miss you so much and long for the day I wake up next to you again.

September 24, 2008

Another long day of moving. We'll start PM classes back up tomorrow. All the TAs thought we'd be able to sleep in since there aren't any AM classes, but if you don't work in the morning, you don't get paid for the day. It's dumb since we work more than any other job. Cleaners work fifteen minutes a day and get the same pay. I honestly don't care, but everyone depends on state aid for support. So we work all day tomorrow.

The bugs have arrived, and they're biters. I can't go outside without ten landing on me. As I was walking around covered in bugs,

Daisy walked up and said, "Don't hate me, but I'm going to Work Release tomorrow." Someone got sent back, and a spot opened. She headed off to feverishly pack. I'm concerned for her as she heads to Work Release, but also worried about Terry. Daisy acted like a buffer between Terry and me. We'll see after tomorrow. School's back in session, and so is Terry.

September 25, 2008

I said goodbye to Daisy this morning. School was a busy distraction, as everyone needed help. I think the days off from moving made the women's brains turn off. There was so much complaining. Another TA quit, and students constantly complain about TAs. We've several new aides in training, but there's a lot to learn. There are only six TAs left. When I was here last time, we had ten aides, and they were good.

I enjoy working with a few aides, but most are very angry and demanding. If you say something they don't like, they'll explode at you. I try to be calm. Mrs. R asked me how I was doing. I could barely keep my eyes open, let alone look her in the eyes. I'm really trying to do my best, but my desire and energy are lacking. She told me to hang in there.

When I got off work, I crashed until dinner. I ate, showered, and now wait for my visit. I'm excited my mom and grandma are coming. I'll have to pull myself together for them. Grandma's really hurting but can be very negative. I love her dearly, and I know she hates this, but it's difficult to hear when I'm already struggling.

I can't wait to see you tomorrow at Visiting. I have to be careful, though; the guard on duty is very strict and rude to me. Becky's father wrote to the Warden after he heard how she talked to me. Becky said it was ridiculous how she treated me. Several who've seen how she treats me told me to grieve the guard. Hopefully, it gets better. It's not easy to be stripped down as it is, but when she's mean, it's belittling.

My cellmate's birthday was today. I shared the plan of salvation, and she shared her story. It was pretty intense, involving drugs, running from police, and someone getting killed.

I just got back from my visit. Grandma also sent a sweet letter that I got in the mail tonight. She wants me out of here so badly. She wrote about last year when I got sentenced. She remembers you handing her the car keys and taking off on foot. She went to the car, and there was my purse, but no Brandy. She said that picture would be forever in her mind. Sigh, I'm so ready to go home.

I had a dream last night that I was pregnant. I told Becky about it. She said she thinks I'll get pregnant at Work Release. Can you imagine that? I certainly hope not. I can't imagine the thought of not getting parole and having to part with my child. I'd go crazy. I honestly have zero idea how women do it when they get locked up away from their children. God definitely knew that'd be too great a burden for me to bear. Anyway, good night, my handsome prince. You're my everything.

September 28, 2008

I walked with Shelly tonight. We talked about how much we love Vala's pumpkin patch. Vala's opened today, and Shelly had a rough morning as she remembered all the trips with her children each fall. She was gripped by the reality she wouldn't be spending this fall with her children at all, let alone at the beloved patch.

She wants me to go to Vala's and take lots of pictures for her. She wants lots of pictures of everything. A picture is worth a thousand words and memories. That feeling intensifies when you're locked up and can't experience it, especially with a sentence like hers. I pray I never lose sight of what life is worth. Staying connected with prisoners would help me keep perspective.

I got to talk to my sister. She went to Homecoming and will send pictures. I really miss getting to talk to her often. It stinks that I only get fifteen minutes to talk each day. My heart sinks when the lady pipes in on my phone call that I only have one minute remaining. I panic and try to become a philosopher and express all my feelings in one minute.

September 29, 2008

I discovered my pay started over at $1.21 a day. When I left, I had the only $3.68 spot. While grading, I talked to another TA. She's been at Work Release before and said violent offenders can't have a vehicle at Work Release. I was crushed as I have no idea what I'll do. I don't know anyone in Lincoln. I'll have to ride a bus and pray I'm not late; otherwise, I can get sent back. I could try to get a sponsor, but who in the world would take me each day? You're the only person I trust, but you're an hour away and working yourself.

The TA continued my spiral of devastation, stating violent offenders rarely get their parole, especially first-eligible parole. That's what the caseworkers said as well. LRC was more optimistic for first parole eligibility, but they don't see that end much. I feel like my heart, hopes, and excitement of Work Release just got squashed.

My charge with its violent tag once again kicks me out of privileges I feel like I've earned. This TA has been back to prison and Work Release several times and will get far more opportunities than I do. I just want my chance. I feel like I have to work harder than everyone else.

I called your mother and vented to her. I felt bad; the poor woman got an earful. Though I was dead tired, I went outside for a walk. I had to get out. Today was awful, and I'm glad it's over. I felt like I got kicked to the curb, and somehow, I literally fell out of my chair at school. I need to sleep. Love you.

October 14, 2008

Same thing, different day, but the cold is setting in. I wish I had my thermals that I had before. These state-issued khakis are paper thin. Cold is a good word to describe what I observe swirling all around me.

I wanted to escape to walk around tonight, but it's pouring out. Shelly showed me her new CD player, so we braved the flood. We popped in her only CD and played Casting Crowns. We found the only spot on the yard we wouldn't get dumped on under a large tree. We sat on a bench watching the rain pour. It was absolutely breathtaking and very calming.

I could've sat there all night. It was the most peace I've experienced while I've been in prison. I can't wait for this flood to be over. I keep thinking; one morning, I'll wake up from a terrible nightmare. Sometimes it just hits me: I'm in prison. I've been away from home for an entire year. It feels like someone stole my heart and continues to shake it violently.

October 16, 2008

I can't believe it. I saw Joanna in D&E. She looked like a ghost. I have so many questions, but I can't talk to her. I can only look with sympathy over the fence separating us. Fear shakes me. She's super sweet and compliant. If she gets sent back, there's no way I'm going to last at Work Release. Women constantly get sent back for violations. My heart aches for her.

October 20, 2008

Joanna hit the yard today. She struggles with an eating disorder. It has attacked in full force since she's been incarcerated. It got so bad at Work Release that she couldn't function. They determined she needed to be on suicide watch rather than Work Release and sent her back to prison.

When I walked up to her, it was like she stared through me. I was excited to see her again, but she wasn't the same. My heart broke for her. I can't imagine what she's been through. She goes to North Hall, but isn't on my wing.

October 22, 2008

I lavished the card you sent. Your words were so encouraging, and I desperately needed them. Thanks for sending money as well. I absolutely hate having to depend on outside money to buy the things I need. I really want to be able to help more. I hate only making $1.21 a day. I'm doing just about what teachers outside do.

I know I sound like a broken record, but school is getting worse. Students constantly crowd around my desk, demanding help. They won't work on their own until I get to them. They throw verbal temper tantrums, upsetting everyone until they get help.

I try to keep my thoughts fixed on what's encouraging. I do love teaching, and I enjoy working with some students. It just seems like the sun that once pierced through heavy clouds can't be seen anymore, and the rain has been pouring for days.

Joanna hasn't been eating. She told me I'm more helpful than her therapists combined. I feel this pressure to do something to fix it. I can't make someone do something, no matter how great my speeches are. Pray I can let go of this burden and the pressure.

I haven't talked to Shelly since her meltdown last night. She's in a bad place. I'm thankful for both my Christian friends, but this week has been a struggle. They're in such deep, dark places. I find myself discouraged rather than prayerful. I need out of this rut, but everywhere I turn, there's misery! Basically, prison stinks!

God's at work. Even through the downpour of rain, the sun is still behind it. Even when we can't see it, the sun's still shining. God is here in the pain and chaos. I'm just ready to move on. Thanks for being my rock and best friend. All my love.

October 24, 2008

I was so discouraged that I cried myself to sleep. At school, a TA pulled me aside and asked, "Brandy, how are you happy all the time? I want to have what you have. What is it?" I was so shocked; I could've fallen over. I'm so miserable right now. God must create some sort of "Happy Brandy" everyone sees instead of the miserable one lurking inside.

I felt like a hypocrite trying to encourage her. I felt empty, with nothing to give, but God took over. He spoke something through me because she said, "That's exactly what I needed to hear." I literally have no idea what I said.

I'd only been at work for an hour, but I needed to talk to you. I took my break and spent the whole time trying to call, but the phones were down. I went to my room and bawled. I just want to hear your voice. I'm so homesick. I finally scraped myself together and went back to school so I didn't get into trouble.

No names were called for Work Release today. Hopefully, no one gets reclassified and turns paperwork in. More than likely, others will go before me. I've had my paperwork in for three weeks.

I ate with Joanna. She had one bite of a carrot and said her stomach hurt. I feel helpless when I look into her lifeless eyes. She's checked out and doesn't respond to half the things I say. She's calling her parents to tell them not to come to visit because she isn't feeling well. She's pushing everyone away. I've never dealt with this before.

The phones were down all night, so I couldn't call you. Joanna wanted to call her parents to cancel, but she couldn't. I walked after she left. I had this feeling I should meet with her after her visit.

After her visit, she came out crying and shaking all over. Her parents were denied custody of her children. Joanna and her husband can't talk to or see their children. Her father's a professor at the University, and both her parents are believers, well-loved in their community. Joanna and her husband received small sentences. They have a lawsuit against a hospital where her baby almost died. Their charge was based on her eating disorder.

I was lost for words. She was already in such a dark place. She said it's pointless to go back to Work Release, but I quickly smashed that theory somehow. God's taking over to speak through me these days.

I'm thankful we did a study together last night. It was about Moses parting the Red Sea. The Israelites were in a seemingly impossible situation between the Egyptians and the Red Sea, and God said not to fear; He would fight for them. God hardened Pharaoh's heart; it was part of His plan. I said, "God hardened that judge's heart, so don't give up hope."

October 27, 2008

While walking, a guard pulled me aside. He said they were meeting to decide what to do about Joanna. He said I've got to get through to her. If anyone can get through to her, it's me. I feel this pressure on my shoulders, but she's mentally checked out. She just stares past me when I talk. All I can do is pray, but I've got a bad feeling about what's next for her.

October 28, 2008

Joanna was sent to Segregation on suicide watch. Mike, she looked like death itself. Something has to give. My back is pressed against a wall. I know that the darkest hour is when the day breaks through. Pray for my endurance.

School's absolutely maddening, and I don't know how much more I can take. The teachers depend so much on me. I understand since they are overworked themselves, but they don't have to go back to live with the most violent students. Pressure, I just feel a ton of pressure.

November 2, 2008

This morning was crash and burn. I felt I was outside of my body, going through the motions. I watched my miserable self walk into a school filled with angry women already lined up for help. They fought over their place in line. I had no idea who was there first. I wanted to exit. Exit. I'm so ready to exit.

I went into the TA room. Everyone's depressed and waiting for Work Release. I wanted to shout at everyone to stop. Mrs. R called me over to her desk and asked what was wrong. All I could do was look at her. She said, "This isn't the same Brandy." I felt heartbroken as I've disappointed her, but at the same time, I feel so numb that I don't care. She has no idea what this is like.

Somehow, I made it through until my morning break. I typically skip break, but not today. I watched myself walk to my building and into my cell. I crumpled myself into a ball on the floor. I tried to console myself, but then I was alone in that place with myself, and cried even louder. I'm just done. I don't know how long I stayed balled up on the floor. A loud voice pierced through. I heard my name paged to the bubble. I've never been paged to control before. I wiped my face and slowly walked to the bubble.

I started to silently panic. Did I get into trouble for not being fully present at work? Dear God, I hope I'm not in some sort of trouble. That's the last thing I need right now.

The guard smiled and handed me a half-sheet of paper. "It's your turn, Reynolds; it's your turn." I couldn't process what she was implying. My puzzled look revealed my confusion, so she continued, "You're headed to Work Release on the next bus."

I don't know what I said. I hope I thanked her. I went back into my room and dropped into the same fetal position I had previously been in. All that came out of me was, "Jesus ... Jesus ... Jesus." I felt like I'd shifted from deepest despair to deepest awe so quickly that it made my world spin.

I managed to get through the rest of my day. I didn't want to rub my half-sheet into any hurting faces. This place has been difficult for everyone lately. I shared my news with Mrs. R, who looked very sad. She's happy for me, but I know how much she leans on me for help. Joanna isn't out of Segregation. She's barely hanging on; how do I leave her? I'm not certain which day I'll leave, but I'll be there by Thanksgiving. *Which.Is.Awesome!*

CHAPTER 17

Lincoln

November 6, 2008

I didn't get much sleep last night. I was up early to finish packing, said my goodbyes, and was called into Intake. We were strip-searched and waited an hour to get packed out. We passed restaurants where everyone grabbed food when they came to the LRC. I'd only pictured these places, so it was surreal to actually see them.

We pulled up to the Work Release building, which resembled a giant dollhouse. Appearances can be misleading. For the next six hours, we waited. Finally, we had orientation, were issued state clothing, visited Medical, and filled out paperwork. We ate a late lunch with men in the same room, which was just weird.

I don't get my job assignment until next Wednesday, which will make for a long week. Most will be assigned a kitchen job. Daisy works in the kitchen, but men work there too, so I'd rather not. I can have three pairs of shoes, but have to wear my lovely state-issued boots to work when I'm on detail.

Work detail is working at this facility or one of the few outside state jobs. We wear state-issued clothing and receive state pay. Everyone starts on detail and awaits the Work Release status. Work Release is authorized by the parole board. Once approved, we apply for jobs and hopefully work in the community. I'll have to work up for furloughs home.

The women's unit is a long hall with eighty-eight women in eleven rooms. Each room has four bunks, two desks, and eight lockers. It's very tight quarters with eight women in each very small room. The overhead light is always off in our room, creating a sense of, "Be quiet." Everyone with a TV plugs earphones into it.

All the women that came today expressed they should've stayed at York. It seems pretty bizarre to say, but it's a big adjustment. The only privilege right away is smoking. There are just more women in your personal space and brand-new ropes to learn. The women here don't like new women coming in. There are men around, creating a whole added level of drama. The two caseworkers for our unit are no-nonsense and don't have the patience to teach newbies the ropes.

I'll get one four-hour shopping pass at the end of the month. I hope to take it around Thanksgiving. I won't get my first furlough until the end of December. I want to be home for Christmas, but I'm trying not to get my hopes up. I'm excited as I get a few things from home, but not as much as LRC.

November 7, 2008

My mind is on overdrive trying to adapt to this new environment. I awoke throughout the night with racing fears, thoughts, and questions about my future. I prayed and surrendered fear by fear, thought by thought, and thing by thing. I begged the LORD to give me peace in return. I woke up and did my devotions with the ability to finally concentrate.

I'm looking forward to our visit tonight. I cannot express how much I appreciate you. I can't wait to get money cleared on my account. Work Release food is by far the worst. I'm dying for a pop— the machine in our dayroom beckons me. We only stay in the room if we're watching TV. If I want to talk, I hit the dayroom. Most play cards and talk.

November 13, 2008

Thank you for bringing me some clothes in. I should've specified not to bring so much pink. My roommate made fun of me all day. I've been nicknamed "Marcia," as in Marcia Brady. I owned it, though. I broke out into some *Brady Bunch* dance moves. They were literally bent over laughing.

We just received a shakedown. I was written up because I had too many socks! I had no idea how many I could have. I just had what we were allowed at York. We just arrived and haven't read the handbook. I've never received a write-up before.

I went to the caseworker's office. She said to consider myself lucky because she never gives verbal warnings. It's a big deal, as I still have privileges taken away. I'll only get a twelve-hour furlough home, instead of twenty-four, for my first month. That's a difference of twelve hours on my first visit home! Pray I don't do anything else wrong that I don't know about.

I'll see a therapist weekly to maintain program/treatment. I'll have to take the 600-question test again. This is my fourth time taking it. I pray I get a good therapist. I'll have to talk to someone new and explain everything all over again.

November 15, 2008

Today I saw the parole board and was classified. I've seen them before at LRC. It's pretty intimidating since they'll be the ones who determine if I get my first parole eligibility next year. They said I'll stay on work details for the next four months until I see them again in March. In March, they reevaluate whether I go to Work Release. I was hoping for sooner than that.

I got my job today. My first assignment was at Nebraska State Penitentiary, working construction with men. Thankfully, my roommate talked to her boss, and I received a job change right away. I'll work in the State Office Building.

Pray Joanna gets here soon. I miss her. Her parents are getting me approval to attend their church. They also dropped off a TV I can use while I'm here. We have to have a clear TV so they can see through it and inmates can't hide anything. It looks weird seeing all the wires inside.

It's been such a long weekend with nothing to do. When I went to the dayroom, I saw Joanna walking in! She looked relieved to see me, and we spent the afternoon walking and catching up.

November 17, 2008

Today was my first day of work detail. I awoke at 3 a.m. and read my Bible until it was time to get ready. We pick up our sack lunch before we head off to work. I peeked inside my sack to find an unlovely chicken salad sandwich of sorts. I'm thankful I tucked away the chips and cheese we had last night at Visiting. I hopped in line to wait for the van transporting us to detail jobs outside the facility.

Everyone smokes in the van, even though they're not supposed to. It was bizarre driving around town. We drove through a neighborhood with busy sidewalks full of people. I hadn't seen life like this in fourteen months. It was wonderful, but it made me homesick.

Our first stop was the governor's mansion. The van goes inside the gates and everything. Three inmates work in the mansion on a special program. It's pretty intensive, and they get interviewed for it from prison. They typically have long sentences and stay at the mansion for several years on their service plan. Christina (TA from York) is there now. The Capitol Building is just a block away, and one man got off. The State Office Building where I'll be working is just around the corner.

I got off the van and stared at a tall building I've never seen before. Regular people walked in and out with normal clothes on. I looked down at my state-issued gray khakis and black work boots. I tried my best to look nice by doing my hair and makeup. Let's face it, though; I stuck out like a sore thumb. There's no doubt where I'm from.

I looked over at the two women from the center, took a deep breath, and walked up the stone steps. The two women started last Friday after the former two had been fired. We walked into the mailroom. It loomed with large machines feverishly working. The women jumped onto their giant machines. The machines are expensive, costing $45,000 a piece.

The mailroom consists of state mail from the entire state of Nebraska. All the mail comes here, and we run it through our machines, applying postage and sealing them. There's a loading dock in the back where it goes out. It's a very boring job. All I do is put the envelopes through the machine, box them, and ship them out.

Only a handful of people work here. They desperately need our help to keep the mailroom buzzing. An older lady next to me was stressed and complained constantly. Another man was loud and overly excited about everything. One gentleman is very nice, but hard of hearing, so it's difficult to communicate with him. There's a girl my age, but I don't feel very comfortable around her. There's a blind lady with her blind Doberman dog. I was excited to pet him as I haven't seen a dog in fourteen months!

A woman said I'm to go help her and led me out of the mailroom. I was relieved to have the break. Ann is about my mom's age, chatty, and a mover. I liked her pace as she took me on a tour of the office supplies she manages downstairs. She enjoys sharing the work gossip in the building. She told me about the man I'll report to. Mr. Henry oversees all the community correction workers. Unfortunately, I've yet to meet anyone with something nice to say about him.

Women hate it here, but he won't let them change jobs. The women get themselves fired so they can change jobs. Ann said every woman who has started here has been fired, totaling fifty this past year. He wasn't here today, so I'm saved from the three-hour speech I'm told I'd have with him. Getting myself fired isn't an option, so I'll tough it out for four months.

Our day was finally over, and we stood outside. The van came and took us back to the center. We work longer hours than most, so we eat in the conference room because it's the men's mealtime. The men stared at us like we were walking down a runway to get food.

Next week is Thanksgiving, so I'll have Thursday and Friday off. I filled out my first pass to see my therapist. I'll go next week and have to miss work. I'm nervous about my first session and think it'll be a rough day. I also filled out a church pass to go with Joanna. Her dad will take us, since he's already an approved sponsor. You can meet us there.

I hope my personal pass goes through soon. I'm so excited to go off with you for a few hours. I know time will fly by. Hopefully, I'll continue getting a four-hour pass each month. I don't know how I'll like this job, but I'll do whatever I have to so I can see you. I love you!

November 22, 2008

The phone system is awful. I'm used to talking to you every morning and starting my day with hearing your voice. I feel disconnected when I don't get that time. No one can hear on these phones. It frustrates me when we try to talk and just never completely understand each other the whole time. I don't want to waste money on phone time.

I walked around listening to the music you made me on my iPod. I thought of all the crap we've gone through. It's a miracle we are still together. We owe it all to God. Our love for each other runs deeper than we knew. No one on this earth could ever love me the way you do. You never gave up on me. Even when you said that you did, I knew in my heart you never would.

We will need each other to get through what lies ahead. Satan knows, too, and relentlessly tries to keep us apart. I never want to go through this heartbreak again. We are not complete without each other. You make me better. God knew what He was doing, even though I not always did. Please keep holding on. Thank you for being my best friend.

November 24, 2008

I met Mr. Henry today. He gave me a list of rules, complete with a PowerPoint presentation. He asked about my job experience. I told him I had my BS degree and was a teacher. He said he was blown away and was certain I don't belong here. He has known me for only a few minutes but can see a vast difference between me and the women over the last decade from corrections.

Mr. Henry's a retired firefighter and received much flack for starting the detail program at the state. He's putting me in the office instead of the mailroom. I'll be the only inmate there and will have my own computer and desk. I'll do all the typing, cleaning, filing, recycling, and errands. I take my breaks in their break room, so I'll be by myself. I'm perfectly fine being alone.

I like having a variety of things to do. I talked to him about the therapy I start tomorrow. He said that's fine, and I'll get half the day off. I'm nervous about talking to a complete stranger tomorrow and dread bringing it all back out again.

I asked about my personal pass with you, but you still aren't approved. I hoped I would get off for the first time with you for Thanksgiving, but at least I can sit with you at church. That'll be my Thanksgiving blessing.

November 25, 2008

A special van was arranged to take me to and from the therapist. I was very nervous about taking the 600-question sexuality test again. When my name was called, I entered my new therapist's office. This is the first time I've seen a male therapist. He was kind, soft-spoken, and much unlike any of the other therapists I've seen. He believes in building others up and focusing on the future. He surprised me by saying he thinks the state needs to reconsider the age of consent. I'll see him each week.

November 27, 2008

Happy Thanksgiving to my best friend. I'm trying to pretend it's just an ordinary day and not another holiday alone. I made a Christmas list that I attached, only because you requested one. My biggest wish is to be home for Christmas. My prayer the entire year has been that I'll be home for Christmas. I need to get ready for my turkey-loaf dinner.

December 12, 2008

We were both frustrated with the phone this morning. I know you can't hear me, but I want to try. I feel so disconnected when we don't talk every day. I couldn't call you back because I ran out of phone time. I wish I could take money out whenever I felt like it, but it's only early Saturday mornings, and I overslept.

You seemed irritated and asked what I spend money on. I live off the $20 a week you send me. After phone time, I buy stamps and snacks for my lunch. The food is absolutely horrible here. I can't bear you getting upset with me. I only make $2 a day working full time. I know I can't do this on my own, and I hate it. I don't like having to depend on you, but what else can I do?

I'm trying to get off next weekend for my pass. It's killing me that I haven't received approval yet. I was the first to submit my paperwork, and you were the first sponsor to get through the class, yet I'm the last person to get approval. Today, I passed out in the shower. I can't take it anymore. The last thing I need is for you to hang up on me.

I feel like I can't tell you when I'm down. You get frustrated with me and pull away, so I try to hold back. I know no one has magic words to make me feel better, but there are words that make me feel worse. I'm already disappointed in myself. I can't stand you being disappointed in me, too.

There are few things I look forward to in my miserable little existence. Getting off to see you was my main goal. That's why I flew through treatment, bit the bullet, went back to prison for three months, and am here. That's why the delay has been so devastating. I've fought and worked through so much to get here. I can't be here one more stupid weekend watching everyone else leave through those doors.

I'm not where I need to be spiritually. I can't figure out how to truly pray anymore. I used to call your mom when I felt like this, but I can't here. I can't talk to anyone on these stupid phones. It's been more difficult being here than I thought it would be. Most women feel the same way. I'm closer to freedom, but also closer to seeing what I don't have. Even when I eventually get away from here for four hours, I'll have to come back. I haven't even been through that yet.

I don't want to make excuses or be weak. I don't want sympathy, but I'm not doing well and feel very guilty. My reactions, words, and thoughts are not in order. My mind is consumed with fears and doubts that I won't get parole. The odds aren't in my favor.

I'm trying to get through this place in one piece. I know you're by my side, but I feel alone. I'm the only person who isn't on medication. Maybe I should go on something, too. I just can't do this anymore.

I feel like hope was always something I had. I dropped it a few times along the way, but I've never been without it for this long and don't know how to get it back. I keep crying out to God, but it doesn't seem like He hears me.

I know I'm not myself right now, but you reminding me of that in words I can hardly make out on that stupid phone only makes it worse. Maybe I should stop calling. You won't get this for two days. I wish I could see you each day. I've been thinking a lot about what happened and have been getting angry. Why does it have to be like this?

I thought I'd rip up this letter like I did the last one I wrote, but I decided you needed to know what's going on with me. Please don't hate me for telling you. I'm sorry I'm like this. I'm sorry I'm not there at home with you. I'm sorry for everything.

CHAPTER 18

Numb

This is, unfortunately, where my prison journal entries end. I went home on Christmas Day for a twelve-hour furlough. I enjoyed Christmas with my family and friends. It was difficult to leave and return to the center, but who'd want to go back to prison after tasting home? I worked up to a twenty-four-hour visit home each month, which was the highlight of work detail.

I was grateful for my job at the State Office Building. My biggest struggle was everyone knew I was from prison. The state-issued clothes did more than just identify me as an inmate. Mr. Henry raved and wrote a wonderful letter about how I was the best community worker he's ever had. The letter was included in my file and given to the parole board. Mr. Henry was recognized for his work of implementing community corrections workers where the state needed help.

The phone system constantly being down completely broke my daily communication with Mike. Our marriage suffered as a result. I worked up to a four-hour shopping pass each weekend, but our time together changed. We went from intentionally visiting to feverishly running around. We constantly checked the time, fearing I was late returning to the center.

March 2009

Winter turned to spring, and I saw the board for a review in March. The board granted me Work Release status. This approval was significant as a registered sex offender. The center gives a mere two weeks to find a job. Being locked up at Work Release as a felon was an extremely difficult task, but I was now a registered sex offender in a new community. I wasn't allowed a vehicle. Drug dealers aren't violent, so they get vehicles. On the other hand, I was considered the worst of the worst, so it was a good old Huffy bike for me. Mike took off work to drive me around, turning in applications. I wasn't getting much response.

I neared the last days of my final week. If I didn't find a job, I would go back on detail and have to wait months before trying again. Mike had burned through all his vacation. I went to HyVee, a Midwest grocery store, and talked to an assistant manager and explained my qualifications for cake decorating. He called the bakery manager, who was on vacation, to hurry the process along. I was down to my last two days when Mike got a call from the HyVee manager wanting an interview.

I was unbelievably nervous as I sat in the interview with a middle-aged man peering down at my application. That application read felon, registered sex offender, and currently living at Work Release. He had a kind smile, but cut right to the chase as he asked why I was locked up. I explained my situation to a complete stranger, yet again. My job duration for the next six months to two years in prison weighed in the balance. I desperately wanted a normal place where I didn't have to wear state-issued clothing that branded me for all to see.

The manager knew several of my references. His wife grew up in the same town I was from. He had talked with my former bakery manager, who spoke highly on my behalf. He then walked me to the bakery. My real test was decorating a cake. I hadn't decorated a cake in years. I gulped, said a quick prayer, and looked for tools. It was a basic iced cake, but I did a tie-dye airbrush he'd never seen and apparently liked by the smile that swept over his face. "You're hired," he said.

God moved a mountain on my behalf. He even offered me more than what my previous decorating job was with a clean record. It was a mere $10 an hour, but more than I'd ever made, especially in prison. I was excited to report to my caseworker that I had found a job. When he heard my news, he looked at me and said, "You're the highest-paid woman here, and you have the worst charge. How is that?"

I just shrugged my shoulders and said, "God?"

August 2009

I was very excited about my new job, but it took me forty minutes to bike to work each way. Mike mapped it all out for me. I truly enjoyed riding my bike. It felt freeing and like a part of me was coming back to life. One morning, on my way to work, I suddenly felt horrible. I was sick to my stomach. I pulled my bike over multiple times to puke. I'd never experienced that before. I was fine one minute and awful the next.

When I got back to the unit, Joanna met me in the bathroom with a pregnancy test. I'd never considered this and felt the ground shift. I'd been going home once a month. I was allowed to be intimate with Mike, but we used protection. The only time I remembered any scares was in June, six weeks prior, on our anniversary, but "there's no way I could be pregnant," I thought.

Joanna handed me the test. I was dumbfounded as I was in the Work Release bathroom, taking my very first pregnancy test. I looked at the strip that revealed my destiny. I showed Joanna, and she declared, "Brandy, you're pregnant!"

After the massive shock impact, fear set in on a deeper level. Fear wrecked a whole new havoc over my mind. No one with my charge had received first-eligible parole in years. I pictured myself having a child while incarcerated and then being forced to send a sweet newborn baby away. The thought of only seeing my baby for a few hours a week for the next two years ran my mind and heart into the ground. I was numb with fear.

Fear grips your heart so immensely that it paralyzes you. My thoughts, perceptions, feelings, emotions, decisions, and actions were skewed. Mike worked two jobs; his letters slowly stopped, and I could never talk to him on the phone.

Looking back at those dark days, God revealed where His love shined through. Joanna's mom was my hero as she drove me to and from work each day. She had a banana and orange juice waiting for me each morning. Joanna's parents also took me to church with them each week. I was thankful I had a job that got me out of the center each day.

September 2009

As my pregnant belly grew, so did the days until it was time for my parole hearing. Everyone said not to get my hopes up. It's difficult to pack as if you'll leave while preparing your heart for the rejection of staying. My numb brain couldn't process anything, so my arms took over and packed myself out.

Several people wrote letters on my behalf and showed up on the morning of my hearing. I was seventeen weeks pregnant as I walked to my hearing. I heard my name being paged to Medical as I walked. I knew the day would come when they'd find out about my pregnancy. I hadn't seen a doctor and was trying to hide my bump.

I walked past Medical and into the room where six men and women would determine my future. I cannot remember what questions they asked. All I remember was a short man declared I'd be paroled that day with a unanimous vote. The tears wouldn't stop. They explained the strict restrictions for the final two years of my sentence while on parole. I'd go directly to my parole officer (PO) after collecting my things.

It's a long walk back to the unit to collect your things to leave while everyone else stays. Everyone acts happy for you, but there's this underlying ache as they remain.

Mike drove me straight to my new PO. There was a new monthly fee of $200 a month for the brick-sized burden that'd be attached to my ankle. This large box would remain with me for the next two years. It needed to be charged nightly, so I'd sleep close to an outlet and let my foot dangle off the bed.

I was given a long list of restrictions. I had to report weekly to my PO, be alcohol and drug tested, couldn't go out of county lines without calling my PO and getting permission, and countless others. By far, the worst was that brick attached to my right ankle. It was difficult to hide for two years, and I felt like everyone could see it as it burned itself into my life. It was a visual reminder of the weight and heaviness of my past still with me. That shackle seemed to define me everywhere I went, and I was afraid. Shame knew me well.

March 2010

My baby doctor saw my monitor every check-up. Having my firstborn should've been an amazing experience, but it was completely embarrassing. My PO came to the hospital to cut off my monitor for my emergency c-section, just to return the next day and reattach it. My daughter had pneumonia and was in the hospital for a week.

It wasn't like I was going anywhere. My PO's comment was, "Well, this's a first." His comment is the story of my life. The doctors and nurses asked questions, especially the nurses who knew me. The more that shame and fear found their home inside, the more I felt a great distance from everyone.

Shortly after, I received a certified mail card to fill out. When I handed the completed card back to the post office worker, he said, "This must be serious." It was. My sex offender registry time of five years as a Level I, "Least likely to re-offend," had changed. There were no longer levels to identify how serious of an offender one was. Under this new law, everyone, even those who'd completed their registration, had to register for twenty-five years or life. I fell under twenty-five years.

Therapists talked about this potential law at LRC. The professionals and law enforcement were against the change. There'd be more sex offenders registering without more law enforcement. Compliant sex offenders that completed their requirements were forced to re-register. Serious offenders fall through the cracks without the levels of risk.

One of the officers said it was a federal government tactic to withhold money until each state would comply. Nebraska was trying to hold out, but here was the letter in my lap. In one letter, I went from having to report for five years to twenty-five years. Twenty-five years of having my picture, information, address, and life open to the public. It'd also be the label that'd reject me from several places, jobs, and traveling. The worst was publicizing my address while I stayed home with my newborn.

⊲⊃⊂⊃⊂

For the next few years, I lived in a fog. I was physically present but just going through the motions. I forgot about the loving God who saved me, gave me a great husband, and loved me. He poured out

His love and grace by working in and through me to reach others in prison. He sent Christians to encourage me through that extremely difficult time, including my husband, who stayed by my side.

I felt so labeled and identified by my past. I was afraid to go to stores, restaurants, or anywhere in public. I wouldn't go to church because everyone knew about my past. Each time I went out of town, I had to call my PO for permission. I nearly had a heart attack when I almost missed the final exit before crossing state lines into Iowa. If I crossed the line, it set my monitor off. I was consumed with pain, bitterness, doubt, and depression. My mind constantly wondered who knew of my past, what they knew, and what they thought about me. I didn't feel safe. I didn't trust anyone, which slowly affected my relationship with God.

Trust is the opposite of fear. The more fear that filled my heart, the less room there was for trust. If I couldn't trust anyone I could see, then how could I trust a God I couldn't see? All the lies that were spoken over me while locked up swirled in my mind.

Slowly, I questioned God. How could God see me any differently than how society did? I was the worst kind of predator. I may not be in prison, but they gave me a monitor to track my every move.

Spiritually, I'd moved a great distance from where I started at the beginning of my sentence. I navigated this transition with a new baby and tried to be a normal wife again. Our marriage was short-lived prior to our two-year separation in prison. Joy was nowhere to be found, and I tried to find it in my own pursuit. Yet, even holding my precious daughter and spending my days with her, I didn't feel the true joy I knew existed flow from my life.

Almost two years into parole, I started a study, "Seeking Him,"
by Nancy DeMoss.[13] I felt God starting a fire inside my cold heart. I'd
never received the healing and restoration I desperately needed for
myself and my marriage.

I spent hours a day biking with my sweet Bella. One day, I was
literally spinning my wheels, and I heard an almost audible voice. It
was like a lightbulb popped on, and I heard, "You know what joy and
peace are like, and you don't have it. Come back to Me."

I looked at my daughter singing to herself in the bike trailer. I
had to get better for her. No matter what she'd ever do, I'd love her
endlessly. Is that what God felt toward me after all I've done?

---

[13] Nancy Leigh DeMoss and Tim Grissom, *Seeking Him: Experiencing the Joy of Personal Revival: A 12-Week Study for Individual and Group Use* (Chicago, IL: Moody Pub., 2009).

CHAPTER 19

Baby Steps

April 2011

Easter was our first Sunday back at church since I'd been home. As we sang the Matt Maher song, his words rang true, "Come awake, come awake, come and rise up from the dead." I was in a dead-like state, and God was shaking me out of it. I felt new life stirring.

Going through my study was a measuring stick to see how far I've drifted. I had many "Oh, yeah, I remember that" moments. Shame and fear had paralyzed me so much that I didn't see things clearly. You don't really see what you've lost until you find it, and I felt like I found an old friend after a long season. Ezekiel 36:26 says, "I will give you a new heart and put a new spirit in you; I will remove from you your heart of stone and give you a heart of flesh."

I was ready to be healed from everything, but there was a lot. I started writing out verses on 3x5 cards as I did in prison. It was an ointment to my broken heart as I memorized so much Scripture during that time. My study challenged me: "Your relationship with Christ will never be any greater than your relationship with His Word." I'd allowed the enemy to be the voice I heard when I wasn't intentionally reading the Bible.

A key thought from the study is, "Whatever it takes to get revival is what it takes to keep it." It took a ton to get life from this dead heart of mine. I'm no longer a prisoner of my past failures. My gracious and merciful God freed me, who pulled off the blinders and allowed me to see through His eyes. He lovingly forgave, restored, and led me from the pit.

I often felt like giving up and shutting the door again. I must stay the path where I've wandered off in the past. Mountain-top experiences come, and I know Satan is squatted in the shadows waiting to attack. I prayed, "Don't let me grow cold again. Allow Your truth to remain. Engraft Your word in my mind, heart, and soul."

I'd taken the wrong paths of what I thought were love, but they led me to lose more of myself. Only God can love me the way I need to be loved. He proved His love by sending Jesus to die a horrible death on a cross bearing all my sins and shame. I desire to wrap my head around that kind of love. How high, deep, wide, and full of that love. I'd experienced that at the LRC. I begged God to let me actually feel His love. He wrapped His arms around me, and I felt Him shield me. He never left me, not in prison, a mental institution, or at Work Release.

I want that connection every day. I have a canyon to be filled and only want Him to fill it. My problem comes when I stop looking to God to fulfill my needs and look to something or someone else. I prayed for eyes to see circumstances for what they were and to rise above what formerly weighed me down. I didn't want to be any kind of prisoner again.

Soon after we started going to church, I joined a study called "Break Free" by Barbara Wilson.[14] Our first group study came, and fear struck me again. My teacher, Suzette, asked us to share why we signed up. We didn't get far when a woman shared she was sexually abused for years. The sharing continued until it was my dreaded turn.

I was heartbroken. I wouldn't be able to stay in my group. The voice of the woman in corrections piped in, "These women will see you as their abuser, and you'll keep them from healing." Through sobs, I shared my story and that I couldn't stay because I didn't want to keep anyone from healing. Suzette's voice pierced through as if it were God Himself: "That's a lie from Satan. You belong here. There's nothing you've done that disqualifies you from being here."

I completed the twelve weeks of intensive study and received much healing. I wanted to give what I'd received, so I started leading groups of my own. I continued growing and followed my mentor to Fort Worth, Texas, to attend Biblical Counselor Training.

Shortly after, my picture was on a Dr. Phil episode that he did on teacher-student relationships. Behind his head were pictures of the teachers. My picture was directly behind his head. I was devastated and cried to Suzette, "I'll never get past this. Why is my sin so public for everyone to see?"

She said, "I feel like what was done publicly, God will restore publicly. God will use this. You are an opportunity for people who are quick to judge to see something different."

---

[14] Barbara Wilson, *Break Free from Your Sexual Past; A Study of Freedom, Forgiveness, Healing and Hope*, 2009.

March 2012

Our church wanted to start a campus church in Fremont. I struggled because I knew many people in town. I felt they'd take one look at me and run for the hills. Suzette asked to pray about it. She raved about her boss, Pastor Mike Wenig, who would be our campus pastor. I cracked open my Bible to where I'd been reading. Jeremiah 29:13–14 radiated off the page: "If you look for me wholeheartedly, you will find me. I will be found by you," says the LORD. "I will end your captivity and restore your fortunes. I will gather you out of the nations where I sent you and will bring you home again to your own land."

As I prayed, I felt God saying it was time to move. "Don't be afraid; just obedient." Being a part of a new campus church launch was a whole new experience. Pastor asked if I'd be open to leading ladies' ministry. Fear gripped my chest as the words fell out of my mouth. "I'll take the broken ones," was my reply. Pastor Mike simply stated, "We are all broken." So I began serving women.

In 2015, we celebrated two years of ministry with a celebration dinner. Suzette read from Joshua, where God told Joshua to be courageous and not fear the giants. She challenged us to ask God what He wanted to break in our lives as she played a song.

The song was Jesus Culture singing, "Break Every Chain."[15] The song repeats, "There is power in the name of Jesus to break every chain." I prayed and asked, "What's the chain that still binds me?"

I felt the sweet taste of freedom from these studies. They were the most powerful instrument of my healing thus far. I heard God say, "What chain still cuts?" As quickly as I asked, I saw the chains of

---

[15] "Break Every Chain," *Awakening - Live from Chicago* (Jeremy Edwardson; Jesus Culture Band/Kristene Dimarco), 2011.

prison. Having to register cut deeply. My mind recalled my recent job at Bath and Body Works.

I had finally mustered enough confidence to apply. The application had a small single line to explain my crime, so I put, "Will explain in interview," like corrections always advised. I opened up about my past and shared everything with the manager. My manager was very understanding, and I got the job.

I was quickly promoted to assistant manager. One morning, after working there for several months, my manager called me into her office. She sat in a chair in the corner, and I heard a voice on the speakerphone asking questions about my crime. He asked why I didn't put my crime on the application. I replied, "There isn't room on the application, and we're told by corrections to write, 'Will explain in the interview,' which I did, and my manager talked to my parole officer."

The voice cut me off: "That's not right; you didn't put it all down because you don't meet the moral ethics of this company. You are fired. You'll be escorted to the door and give her the keys to the store."

Everyone stared as my bawling manager led me to the door, sobbing, "I'm so sorry." I had to report my job termination to the Sheriff as a part of my sex offender registration that same day.

The song was almost over. What could lift that kind of chain? The only thing that could free me from all the restrictions was a pardon. I wasn't supposed to pursue a pardon until ten years after my parole. It had only been four, but I felt God tell me to start.

It took over a year to complete the paperwork and collect a hundred character-reference letters. The application only called for two letters, but I wanted as many as I could get. It would be a miracle if I got the pardon at all, let alone early.

September 2013

The fire continued growing as I finally said "Yes" to my friend's relentless begging to join the local Mothers of Preschoolers (MOPS) group. I dragged my feet in going to MOPS for a long time because I was afraid of the community realm. I was in a community I not only grew up in, but that now labeled me. I didn't think I needed a social outlet group like MOPS. I had friends from church, but to appease my begging friend, I joined. My greatest gain was the break I received from my two children who were in childcare. The newest Reynolds was my first son, Tytus. He was my redheaded wonder. Mike worked long hours, and I didn't have help with the kids. I quickly developed friends at my table and enjoyed many of the speakers who shared their life stories.

Vickie, our leader, called me toward the end of my first year, saying she wouldn't be able to lead the group the following year. Several women had suggested I lead. There were plenty of other equipped leaders in our group. I didn't want to share about my felony. I planned to skip the leadership meeting for the new year, but everyone kept reminding me and I thought I'd just sit through it.

I dragged myself to the meeting and slumped down on the couch. There were about ten that listened to Vickie share there wouldn't be a group the next year if they didn't find a coordinator. After the long silence, she turned to me and said, "Brandy, several have wondered if you'd be willing to lead."

I shook my head, "No," and all eyes remained on me.

I felt warm and tingly, like I often do when God asks me to share. I thought, "No way, LORD, I'll share my story in Bible study for others to heal, but not in the community. It's not safe. These women are put together, key members of the community. One of them can lead."

The feeling to share intensified, so I obeyed. My story came flowing out of me like a fountain. I tried to highlight why I wasn't qualified to be this leader they thought I was. Then I added, "This is my very first year of MOPs, and I have no idea what I'm doing." I figured that'd do it. The whole room was completely silent.

Vickie broke the silence: "That's exactly why you should lead."

I was shocked. She didn't understand me correctly. The meeting continued, but I couldn't even focus. I was thoroughly confused. When everyone stood to leave, I was ready to bolt, but Vickie cornered me. "We'll have to talk to the pastor and make sure everything is good to go. I'll talk to him and set it up, and I can go with you."

I mumbled something about praying about it.

For the next few days, I struggled with the Lord. I really didn't want to put myself into this position of leadership open to the public. He reminded me that He gave me leadership gifts, and they weren't mine to keep to myself. I reminded Him I was already leading studies and ladies' ministry, so why lead another thing in the community?

Vickie said we'd be meeting with the pastor. I thought about how the last time I shared my past with a pastor, it didn't go so well. I felt God say, "Keep walking until I close the door." I was certain the door would close after talking to this man.

As we introduced ourselves, my eyes wandered behind his head. Hanging on the wall behind him was a plaque of his certification from Southwestern Theological Seminary, the exact place I'd received Biblical Counselor Training. It gave me peace to unfold my story. The pastor concluded that I had his vote, but the church would vote as well. If approved, he'd contact MOPS International for approval. He also reached out to an attorney for legal approval. My relief from sharing quickly faded at the list of hoops to jump through. I heard, "Keep walking until I shut the door."

One woman from MOPS wasn't happy the church was interested in me. She posted my mugshot on my Facebook page. When I saw it, I panicked. Why does God want me to lead this? I don't want this opposition. I've had enough to last a lifetime. I'm just trying to be obedient. I heard, "You're an opportunity for people that judge to see things differently."

I called Vickie to sweetly decline, but she cut me off. The church voted for me to lead. The hired attorney said I was legally clear to be around children and lead mothers. Her words brought tears to my eyes. Why would the church hire an attorney to ensure a registered sex offender leads a nonprofit ministry? The pastor's words from our meeting came to mind, "We don't answer to this world. If we did, this church wouldn't be here. We answer to God."

I was certain MOPS International wouldn't want their name associated with my label. This would be where the door shut. The MOPS theme for the year was released, "Be you, bravely." I laughed, for if this wasn't brave, I don't know what was. All the labels and rap sheet aside, the Brandy before prison would have led a group. I was the president of my collegian at college and loved it. I hadn't thought about that Brandy in a long time. She felt dead. God reminded me of the gifts He gave me of leading, teaching, and encouraging others.

MOPS left the final decision to the host church. The church had already approved. That was it; I'd be the coordinator. That first meeting was both frightening and exhilarating. I bravely shared my testimony with all my failures. I wanted them to hear everything from me. I was blessed to have an incredible leadership team rally alongside me.

After sharing that first meeting, a woman from the church came up to me. She said her husband was Officer Reynolds. Years ago, he came home from working a long day transporting a young lady to prison in York. He told her, "God showed me there's something different about this girl, and we need to pray for her." With tears pouring down her face, she said they never stopped praying for me. MOPS became my safe place where I belonged, was loved, and was desperately needed.

Al and Nadine Peters, who lead Bible studies in York, contacted me about the need for Angel Tree. Angel Tree is a ministry that allows inmates to sign their children up to receive gifts on their behalf through a local church. I saw firsthand how Angel Tree impacted Daisy in prison. The church bought her children presents that said they were from her. Her letter included pictures of her children and a message from them. Daisy sobbed, "When I get out, I'm going to take my children to that church."

The Peters said there was a need for a coordinator in Nebraska. Pastor Mike was in, but we needed help. I talked with the youth pastor of the main campus. They looked for a Christmas project and had a hundred youths. I relented to talk to the youth pastor, but he needed to know my story. His willingness to help with his posse of youth surprised me. They raised money to buy each child a Bible. We promoted the angels on trees for the congregation to pluck and sponsored 250 children that year. I volunteered full time for months, calling to verify information, make tags, collect gifts, and organize one banging party. There were cookies, activities, singing, a photo booth and a message.

The night before the party, I panicked. It was as if, in my business, I'd forgotten the lies. "You are a sex offender partnering with youth to teach children." It wasn't illegal, but I could't breathe. I called the officer I reported to in tears.

He spoke calmly, but sternly, "Brandy, are you asking me if it's okay that you minister to a bunch of kids at Christmas time? There's nothing wrong with you being around children. You are covered."

I could breathe again. The party was a hit, and the following year, we partnered with an intercity church serving 450 children.

Things were going well, and I loved serving in multiple ministries. I longed to hear from the pardon's board, but thrived in the meantime. We were blessed to have our second son, Jacob, in 2015, right before Christmas. Bella was almost five years old, and we prayed about where to send her to school. The public school system said I had to verify each time I stepped on school grounds. If staff knew my label, eventually, students would as well. Picturing my little girl being harassed wasn't an option. Where would we send her? We were running out of options.

CHAPTER 20

Rejection

March 2015

We made an appointment with the principal of a Christian school. The principal listened, sympathized, and even shared some of his own struggles. He was for us, but the board needed to vote. It was me against another board. I submitted character letters, including ones from the Sheriff and Todd's brother, whose children attended the school.

Months later, we finally heard from the principal. If we sent Bella, I wouldn't be allowed to step foot on school grounds. This was worse than the public school. I couldn't drop her off or pick her up from school, attend activities, or attend conferences. The law doesn't say I'm not allowed in certain places or can't be around children.

I was frustrated the church school responded with more rejection than the community. I felt the familiar knife in my heart twist. Why do some Christians accept me and others reject me? I led

MOPS and women's ministry. I wasn't a threat, and it's not against the law. It felt that Christians judged me worse than society. It was clear homeschooling was the only option for our family.

Two years later, I received a letter from our YMCA. They had revoked my membership. Registered sex offenders could no longer be members. I didn't want to go and share my past again, but my children were involved in activities. It was important to have this social outlet as we homeschooled.

Mike and I set up a meeting and poured our hearts out to the director. He was compassionate and certain we'd be the exception, as none of the other hundred sex offenders had set up to meet with him. Months later, the main board denied my reinstatement, stating, "If we let one of them in, we let them all in." I was thrown into a labeled box once again.

I sent my pardon application a year later and entered the Capitol. My anxiety was through the roof as I entered the tightly packed chamber room. When my name was called, I walked down the aisle and faced the board consisting of the governor, secretary of state, and attorney general. I tried to explain my reasons for submitting early, but the board said, "While it's a very compelling story, it's too soon."

I was told to resubmit in two years. Two years came and went, and I resubmitted. Soon after, I received another rejection letter. Rejection was the word that loomed over my head. It slowly dragged the life out of me.

The rejection monster grew when my Facebook account was deleted. Ten years of my family pictures, skincare and cake business were gone. I felt cut off from another part of this world due to my label. I didn't remember this rule when I signed up a decade ago, but at some point, it was instituted. I tried to get access to get my pictures and contacts, but was denied. I Facebook died.

"I'm never enough." That lie was my constant enemy. I tried to rise above it, but the pain continued festering. It dragged me back to the real chains that cut. Up to this point in my life, I had rarely drunk alcohol. But I found myself around different circles of Christians who drank. I found myself trying what they drank and enjoying it too, but what I really enjoyed was how life felt easier when I drank.

October 2019

I was asked to volunteer in the children's ministry at church. My friend was the children's director and knew about my past. She was desperate for help and had already asked Pastor Mike, whom I worked with for the past seven years. I had avoided being with children because I wanted to protect myself from any false accusations, but I felt comfortable with my pastor, who knew my past and supported me.

My class was small and consisted of two of my own children and a few others whose mothers had gone through my studies. I taught with another friend in the room with me once a month.

I had served in this ministry for several months when our campus added an associate pastor. I reached out to his wife and shared my past, as she was the new children's leader. We became friends, and she volunteered at our MOPS group. I didn't realize she had been looking for a children's leader to replace her. This new leader was completely new to church and heard me share my past in Bible study.

Shortly after, the new pastor's wife said they needed to share something with Mike and me. She and her husband had been to some big meeting at the main church. It came to the attention of the big church pastor that I was a registered sex offender.

I thought, "Okay, no big deal. He should've already known about my past. I've been leading the ladies' ministry for our campus for the past seven years. He promoted Angel Tree from the pulpit. He even sent me a Bible when I was incarcerated. All the other pastors knew."

The big church pastor consulted an attorney and gathered leadership for a huge meeting. Everyone had to write statements about what they knew of my crime. The pastor hashed over my past without talking to me. Pastor Mike was outraged and refused to deliver the news to me: I could no longer serve in the children's ministry. I hugged them goodbye and sat in shock.

This isn't against the law. Thinking about the leaders going over my past cut deep. This church has trained me that our stories are of utmost importance and need to be kept confidential. The thought of leaders being required to dissect my past without my knowledge broke me. That goes against everything that a church should be. Their mission statement is, "CrossRoads groups give men and women a safe, confidential place to walk in a Gospel-centered community and pursue redemption in Christ."

Mike asked if we wanted to continue attending. The thought hadn't even crossed my mind. Mike and I served in various ministries within the church. Then I thought of taking my children into the classrooms. I'd have to send them into a room I wasn't welcome in. I received this from an associate pastor I barely knew. I saw a line drawn in my own church. I was cut off yet again.

The next week, Pastor Mike posted a job update, "Left position at the church." After his resignation, our satellite church was in great upheaval. No one in the church knew why he resigned. He directed questions to the main church pastor, who came to our campus church to answer questions. I couldn't stomach attending but was filled in on the bloodbath afterward. Though it was about our beloved campus pastor's resignation, my past quickly came to the surface. Those that didn't know about me at my own church now did.

I hated having anger toward a pastor. Is this why I struggle with trust? Since childhood, I looked to the church as my relationship with God. I knew Him as my own, but it felt contingent on my relationship with Christians at church. It feels so heavy, and I don't know how to break it.

I tried to stay connected, but everyone was hurting. It felt like a huge breakup. I avoided my own emotions and thought instead about Pastor Mike. He should've received a retirement party. My husband and I coordinated the party and threw him the party he deserved.

During the party planning, I didn't calculate how difficult attending would be. It was apparent how much he was loved by the packed-out room. I walked into the room filled with countless people that now knew the worst about me in the worst possible way. I broke up this band of believers. I wanted to run. Instead, I found myself in the corner, trying to quiet my kids as everyone shared their hearts about Pastor Mike. The rest of the children flocked to me and my children. This tragedy stemmed from my serving in the children's ministry. Here I was, watching their children, while they fellowshipped for the last time.

I slowly faded into the shadows. This is what they think of me after all the years I spent doing what God asked. This is what I am. I will always be a reject, an outcast, and never belong. Another denial letter from the pardon's board followed. The shadows offered me an easy out rather than working through what God could possibly do with the surmounting rejection, so I numbed my brain instead.

November 2019

I really liked the church we had went to in September for our nephew's baby dedication. I remembered thinking if we weren't in ministry, we would've considered trying it. We were in that position, but the thought of church frightened me after the previous rejection.

I prayed God would give affirmation if this was the place. That first Sunday, we drove into the parking lot, and I saw a sign that read, "You are welcome here." That gave me the courage I needed to step into church again. The pastor started a series called "Brand New." Behind his head on the screen, it said, "BRAND." I figured the picture would change like it usually does, but it didn't. I thought it was odd that my name was behind his head. "Brand" is what my dad calls me.

God was really going to have to spell it out for me, so I asked Him to show me more. Suddenly, the episode on Dr. Phil popped into my mind. On his show, my picture was behind his head. Here I sat with my name behind the pastor's head. This was my affirmation. Mike saw it as well and took a picture. The service ended, and the invitation came. As people walked forward to receive Christ, a song began playing. It was the same song I heard during the worship. Tears flowed as I sang the song "This Is a Move."[16]

One Sunday, shortly after, there was a meeting to discuss a new campus launch. I was shocked to learn they were starting a campus in my town. My heart sank as I didn't want to walk through it all again. I was encouraged that our campus pastor, Robert Wilson, was also a felon.

In the same week, I learned my former church closed their doors for good and our new church would be launching as they'd secured a building. I found it affirming that my former church closed the same week as this new opportunity was before me. Then I learned that our church would be in the old Oriental Trading Company call center building. I had worked at OTC throughout high school. In fact, my cubical was where the welcome entry is now located. It felt like God orchestrated all the details just for me, but I know that's just the way He works.

I battled staying sober. One Sunday, I looked down at my hand in worship. I had a blister on my right hand from accidentally burning it on the stove when drinking. That hand tries to drown my pain with alcohol. I dreamed about a venomous snake biting me on that same hand. Something in worship invited me to lift that same hand. *This*

---

[16] "This Is a Move," (Tasha Cobbs Leonard), 2019.

hand is supposed to be raised, holding Yours. This place Satan is trying to destroy me; You mean to bring life.

My punishment continued with a pardon covered with dust on the desk of the governor. I gave my life, served my time, volunteered where You called, but it's never enough. Yet, You say I am enough. I know You freed me because of Jesus. Why is the voice of the law, society, and others so great? I've been sitting in years of chains. I can't shake the weight in the wait.

Jeremiah 30:8 says, "I'll break the yoke from your neck, and I will tear off your bonds and force apart your shackles; and strangers will no longer make slaves of the people." My yoke is bondage, oppression, and slavery. Strangers do enslave me. Society labels and brands define me by putting me in a box with the worst. Murderers are seen in a better light than I am. There are bars everywhere I go. I feel bars when I pass my childhood church where I accepted Jesus, served, sang, and taught others.

I feel bars at my former high school. The same stage I performed on is where Bella has her dance recitals. I can't attend unless I get permission from the superintendent. He asked for endless details of my life, all because I just wanted to watch Bella dance.

Society screams, "Stay away from us. You're not welcome. You are a pedophile." That word makes me want to die. I can feel a hot blade pierce through my heart. The same heart that loves children and taught them well.

I feel bars at the YMCA where I can't be an exception to their rule. God forbid if they let "One of my kind." I feel bars when I see a Facebook app or hear conversations taking place in a world I cannot see. Ten years of pictures of my family, cakes I made for my children, conversations, and interactions with groups God asked me to lead. Cut off again with another part of me taken away. My online business is now stripped away. Stripped, I had to be strip-searched all the time. My body was naked and open to see each time a blessing walked through the metal bars. How could there be anything left? Everything gets taken away.

Rejection and isolation are my norm. I was isolated from everyone in Segregation when I first entered prison. I was too bad to be even around violent criminals. Feeling cut off has triggered prison. I spent two years on intensive parole with a giant box attached to my ankle. I couldn't go underwater, take a bath, go outside county lines, or be free after delivering my sick daughter. I felt the bars for the first year of her life. I lived in fear that year. It should've been a joy, but that, too, was stripped away—a visible reminder of how bad I am.

I can't leave the state without telling someone that doesn't even know me. I sit here cold, much like my first night after my sentence. *When will You tear off my bonds? When will foreigners no longer enslave me? Harder yet, if that day ever comes, will I be able to receive it? Will I want to go places that once rejected me? Will it always be a reminder of my past? How do I get past this?*

May 15, 2020

I finished reading Psalm 69 and sobbed. I am broken. My shattered heart numbs itself daily. I'm an empty shell trying to pound out another day for my children and family. It's difficult to admit, so I bust myself to stay busy. I wanted to go to counseling to work through all this, but Covid hit—no more gatherings. I could've found help despite my circumstances, but my coping mechanisms had already kicked in. I just want to escape far from the faces of my past.

Judgmental Christians and the rejecting society continue oppressing me. I feel like it's me against the entire world—all except my family and the band of women from my MOPS group. I wouldn't be alive if they didn't surround me. I don't enjoy God like I once did. I somehow missed the mark, missed the cut. The world wants me out and exposed for all to see. They violated me, like when I was strip-searched, to my utter humiliation, each time I wanted to see Mike. I don't know how to undo it all in my mind.

God gave me a picture of the Tree of Life. I stand at the entrance, afraid to go in, but my family and friends block my escape. So, just as I continue living for them, I step inside. The massive tree has a wooden staircase that swirls all the way up to the top. I'm enclosed in a sparkling white gown. I peer down, and there's Jesus waiting to dance with me. My heart longs for this, but I don't know how to dance with Him. I'm so broken, undeserving, and wounded.

I don't know how to continue in my picture. I never quite get to Him. He's given me other pictures over the years. I see an ocean and, like Moana, "It calls me." I'm on a white horse wildly running along the shore. My long, flowing white dress hits the water's edge behind me. I gaze at the water, and there He is again. My Jesus. He wants me to come to Him. My eyes are set on a long pier. I ride to it and leave my horse behind. I run toward Him. Suddenly I'm swooped up in a swing encirclement with colors I've never seen. I'm raised high above the water, suspended in the sky, with an incredible view. I'm away from everything and filled with immense joy. I look back at the shore, and masses of people walk out to the ocean. I hear that word so many times, "masses." I feel like maybe when I finally get this "thing" out of me, the masses will come to Him. That image keeps me going on the days I struggle most.

Another picture is as if I'm Tarzan swinging on vines through a jungle, quickly trying to escape. I stay busy, swinging as fast as I can. I'm desperate to see the blue sky of my exit, but all I see is the next vine. I feel in control as I grab the vine and swing to the next. It feels good, but I still can't manage to escape. I peer below. On beautiful sparkling water, Jesus stands next to a small boat with his hand extended. I finally take time to look at where the stream leads. It empties into the ocean, my way out. He speaks to my heart, "My way is easy, My burden is light." Why can't I just sit with Him?

The last I saw, Jesus was robed in white in a lake, splashing and having fun with my friends from Bible studies. He locks eyes with me and waves me to join. My eyes break, and I see another friend wanting to join but staring at her feet in despair. I grab her and toss her in, seeing the smile born in her heart. He locks eyes again and says, "Join us."

My heart responds, "No, I'll just find them and toss them; that's my part." He wants me in the water, so why can't I move?

Why can't I see the end of the scene He wants for me each time? I read my Bible, pray, and do studies; it's as if I almost get it but fall short. The world's voice over me grabs me back. They define me, label me an outcast, and reject me. Just like my childhood church and our church we served in the past eight years.

October 31, 2020

I hit another two-day restoration event at church. I'm addicted to alcohol. I can't lean on something that's destroying me. I want to be well. In restoration, we walked through a lamenting process. We were invited to sit in the pain we've been avoiding. This was a very difficult activity for me. In fact, I escaped at break time and loaded up on Fireball shooters. Not my best plan.

I live a very busy life as a stay-at-home homeschooling mom of three kids with three "side hustles," as Dave Ramsey likes to put it. When I get downtime, I drink. I opened my Recovery Bible to Lamentations, and the theme reads, "When we harden ourself to the pain involved in the grieving process, recovery cannot take place."

I've allowed myself to get hard, and in the process, I'm losing myself. After I dumped a crazy amount of Fireball down my throat, my husband told me he wanted his wife back. I'd like her back too, but what does that look like? Though I was hungover, I returned to the conference on the second day.

My Bible reads our emotions are a gift. Nothing is closer to our core than our emotions. If we develop a pattern of hiding our feelings and emotions, we lose a sense of who we are before God. I've lost the sense of my identity in Christ as His child. I know it in my head, but all the lies from the enemy cloud my heart. I constantly think of how society labels me and how the church (once again) treated me.

I can't do this on my own. The enemy has wreaked havoc in my life. Lamentations 2:13, "What can I say about you? Who has ever seen such sorrow? O daughter of Jerusalem, to what can I compare your anguish? O virgin daughter of Zion, how can I comfort you? For your wound is as deep as the sea. Who can heal you?" He calls her "daughter "and "virgin." That's still her identity, despite her behavior.

I think back to when I was a child swinging alone, singing to myself. I'd travel to a church where I'd learn of Jesus, but didn't measure up. I tried to find the security I desperately longed for in a marriage that shattered a few short months after it began. The enemy targeted, baited, and almost took me out. I came to terms in prison but struggled with the pressing anxiety of going back to a society that labeled me the worst. I have suffered rejection after rejection. I have an amazing family and friends that have survived the worst with me. I would die for God. Why can't I truly live for Him?

How can God comfort me in this? My wound is as deep as the sea, the massive sea I gravitate toward. Why can't I see Him as my massive God? Why can't I swallow that God's in control, my defender, and for me?

Mike wants me to write a letter to read to myself when I'm tempted to take that first drink. It frustrates me that I have to let another thing go. Another place that's off limits for me that once was enjoyable. I have another weakness open for people to judge. Another thorn that pierces my flesh. God, give me words.

> Brandy,
>
> You are more than this. This will not give you what your heart truly needs. You need Me to weather this storm. Come with Me instead. Don't look at what they are drinking, or the bottles on the shelf. They never satisfy.

Look in My eyes and draw in My spirit. I promise life, and you know that you were close to death.

It may feel strong, but that was fire you poured down your throat, coating the pain for but a moment. Give Me the pain—all of it. I can handle it all. That way will lead to your fall and you know how close you were. I know, I know, this life isn't fair. This isn't what I had planned, sweet girl. My sweet little girl. I know, I know. Let it out, but only let Me in. I promise to give you what you need each time you take My hand instead of that drink.

Let Me lead you to what I have. Sit here by My side. Just sit and rest. You are My daughter, perfect in My eyes. Come sit, wear your crown, your gown and rest. My mansion is secure, safe, and you are Mine. I sit on the throne as the King of Kings and Ruler over all. Shut them all out, for it will never matter when we spend our eternity together. I have a plan for all this pain, so give it all to Me. Hold nothing back, including this useless drink that will start you wanting the next one and never feel full. Give it to Me, and I will give you something better. Drink Me in instead, little one. Choose Me, for I have chosen you.

I did well that fall and into the Christmas season without drinking. Being sober left me feeling all the big feels again. I felt like I'm doing it all with little help from everyone. From homeschooling, cooking, cleaning, being the one everyone goes to for anything, side jobs, leading a nonprofit, and being a wife, sister, daughter, and friend of many.

New Year's Eve came, and I tried to balance drinking with a restricted regimen. The problem was I could never control it. It controlled me. Ephesians 4:1, "Therefore I, a prisoner for serving the

Lord, beg you to lead a life worthy of your calling for you have been called by God." When I feel enslaved to drink, make me a prisoner of the next word from You.

Ephesians 5:18, "Don't be drunk with wine, because that will ruin your life. Instead, be filled with the Holy Spirit, singing psalms and hymns and spiritual songs among yourselves, and making music to the Lord in your hearts." I'm claiming this as singing has been birthed from the pain in my life, from the swing outside in a lonely childhood, to singing to myself in prison, to the worship team at church. Let my song rise above the temptation, and joy reside where pain once did.

CHAPTER 21

She Arose

I began attending a support group called Celebrate Recovery. CR is for anyone with a hurt, habit, or hangup to walk through a Christ-centered twelve-step program. The addiction had attached itself far beyond what I thought. My husband reached out to our campus pastor for help. Pastor Robert and his wife, Joyce, invited us to pray with them.

I walked into his office on March 31, 2021, scared to death. I was sick of being sick and had to meet with yet another pastor. Pastor Robert was different, as he knew what it was like to be behind bars. However, he was walking in freedom, and I was not. My family has every thread of sin one can commit, deeply rooted in generation after generation. I was the first Christian in my family. Satan targeted me in full force. They prayed God would break the power of sin in my life that streamed through generations before me.

As they prayed, I felt myself physically rising from my hunched fetal position of shame. I felt lighter, as if weight was lifting from my back, shoulders, chest, and head.

They called me to remember who I am in Christ. I felt captivity shaking off and rising from the depths. I felt the love and favor of God. I heard God call me a daughter of Zion. I've been held captive by the lies for far too long. I've partnered with the enemy by agreeing with him about who he said I was. God created me, so He gets to tell me who I am. God loves me no matter what I do and died for me. It was by His stripes cutting into his flesh that I received healing. He can do this. He can do anything. It'll be difficult, but living like this is killing me.

The next morning, I awoke and heard God declare again, "Daughter of Zion," and I reached for my Bible. Isaiah 52:1–2, "Wake up, wake up, O Zion! Clothe yourself with strength. Put on your beautiful clothes, O holy city of Jerusalem, for unclean and godless people will enter your gates no longer. Rise from the dust, O Jerusalem. Sit in a place of honor. Remove the chains of slavery from your neck, O captive daughter of Zion."

"Wake up! Wake up!" I heard the same thing years ago, Easter Sunday, when God shook me back to life. When had I allowed fear to paralyze me again? The verse said to put on clothes of strength. I needed strength to make it through day one of staying sober. I typically don't make it far. In the past, I'd make it a couple months until another rejection letter stormed my world. How did these chains lock around me again? I was determined to leave my captivity.

The hardest year in your recovery is the first. Getting through holidays, celebrations, and life without a drink in your Yeti. It's the absence of comfort. One day at a time, one moment at a time, one celebration at a time, one event at a time, one disaster at a time. Putting one foot in front of the other without the former crutch. I was learning how to walk again in freedom.

It's vital to get quiet time with my Bible and a devotional book each morning. After school, I'd put in my earbuds and jog while listening to worship music. That time away has been my sanctuary. I intentionally connect with God and felt His spirit give me the power to finish my day. Temptations became fewer as my presence with God grew.

CR has been a great support. We enter a safe space to be honest without feeling judged. We sing, listen to a testimony, and read Scripture. We celebrate each other's milestones of sobriety with a chip that reads, "My grace is enough for you."

As 2 Corinthians 12:7–10 says, "To keep me from becoming proud, I was given a thorn in my flesh, a messenger from Satan to torment me and keep me from becoming proud. Three different times, I begged the Lord to take it away. Each time he said, 'My grace is all you need. My power works best in weakness.' So now I am glad to boast about my weaknesses, so that the power of Christ can work through me. That's why I take pleasure in my weaknesses, and in the insults, hardships, persecutions, and troubles that I suffer for Christ. For when I am weak, then I am strong."

Like Paul, I asked God to remove my thorns, but God hasn't yet. If I forget who God is and His true character, then I slowly listen to lies and doubt God. God loves me; He's for me, and I'm forgiven and precious in His eyes. I'm His dearly beloved child that He bled and died for. He allows this thorn to continue cutting me for a reason. God's grace is enough, and because He is enough, I'm enough. The more I tune into God, His word, and the songs He sings over me, the less I hear from my enemy.

Zephaniah 3:16–20. "Cheer up, Zion! Don't be afraid! For the LORD your God is living among you. He is a mighty savior. He will delight in you with gladness. With his love, he will calm all your fears. He will rejoice over you with joyful songs. I will gather you who mourn for the appointed festivals; you will be disgraced no more. And I will deal severely with all who have oppressed you. I will save the weak and helpless ones; I will bring together those who were chased away. I will give glory and fame to my former exiles, wherever they have been mocked and shamed. On that day, I will gather you together and bring you home again. I will give you a good name, a name of distinction, among all the nations of the earth, as I restore your fortunes before their very eyes. I, the LORD, have spoken!"

God's ways are higher than mine, and His timing isn't my own. The key is not to turn away from God when it gets painstakingly hard. I tend to go into self-protection mode. I don't feel like I had a safe place to take my problems, so I relied on myself. I still wrestle with trying to "fix" things myself. If I can't fix it, I try to numb my pain.

Psalm 46:10, "Be still and know that I am God." When we forget He is God alone, we are held captive by another lesser god and thus a prisoner. I've experienced both a literal prison and an imaginary prison of my own making. We are robbed of peace when we are a prisoner. Peace flows when we are still in the presence of God.

My identity as a child was never fully instilled. I looked to someone else who could tell me who I was and if I was truly loved. I found Christ at a tiny church. I desperately clung to that church, to its steeple, and, unfortunately, all the little people. In my eyes, they were big and important people. People I put on the same shelf as God. But when a broken girl revealed her brokenness, broken believers banished her. The law banished me thereafter. I thought God did, too. After all, they were on the same shelf.

January 1, 2022

This New Year's was different, as I celebrated nine months of sobriety. Celebrating without drinking nagged at me. When thoughts attack, I have to switch gears immediately. If I cater to the thought, my mind dwells on it, and the thought seeps into my heart, which chews on it. It's poison I digest, and then I tank. I must pray, take each thought captive, and move on to something positive. As 2 Corinthians 10:4–5 says, "We use God's mighty weapons, not worldly weapons, to knock down the strongholds of human reasoning and to destroy false arguments. We destroy every proud obstacle that keeps people from knowing God. We capture their rebellious thoughts and teach them to obey Christ." I picture myself taking that temptation and laying it at the feet of Jesus. I need to slay the thought before it slays me.

I recently received another rejection letter in the mail. We sponsor a child in Honduras paying for school, food, and medicine. The new policy stated that registered sex offenders can't sponsor children. My Bella wrote this little girl. We were heartbroken.

Another rejection letter on the stack. Will I allow rejection permission to hammer another nail into my heart? It's like the song, "Come Thou Fount of Every Blessing."

"Prone to wander, Lord, I feel it, prone to leave the God I love."

But I pray, "Here's my heart, oh take and seal it."

Proverbs 4:23 says, "Above all else, guard your heart, for everything you do flows from it."

I reached out to a friend who encouraged me. Ultimately, what I allow this letter access to is on me. I ran and poured my pain out to God. He showed me this was the first rejection I have received in several years where I didn't drink to drown the pain out. That felt liberating.

March 31, 2022

I'm one year sober today. I never thought I could go this long without drinking a single drop. This past year has been absolutely freeing. It feels like I've awakened from a long, foggy dream. I'm alive, present, and aware. I'm no longer captive by addiction, pain, or sickness.

My relationships have changed as well. I feel more assertive than before, sharing my feelings, exercising my boundaries, and saying "no" to things I didn't want to do. Before, if I helped someone by doing something I didn't want to do, I'd reward myself with a shot of vodka. It seemed to give me what I needed to do what others were asking of me. What a vicious, pointless cycle of chaos.

Mike surprised me with flowers. Hanging from the vase were all twelve of my chips, colorfully displaying my victories, the 365 days of working through pain, temptation, addiction, and fire. Praise God; I'm on this side! Mike surprised me with a dinner with friends. I'm grateful. Most don't stick it out for the long haul. Several friends and family members certainly haven't. It's difficult to see someone you love struggling so much.

Later, I stood in line at the gas station waiting to buy my diet Mountain Dew. The lady at the counter said, "Is there anything else I can get you?" They don't normally ask if there's anything behind the counter they can get me. She doesn't know the countless wars I've had in my head at this very counter about whether or not to get vodka shooters behind her.

"I'm all good," is my reply. Praising Jesus that I'm all good! I walk out free.

April 20, 2022

After CR, Mike, our two boys, and I took our two Yorkies, Rocky and Ruby, for a walk. I was high on life as I looked at their little smiling faces rattling on about their day. We turned the corner and heard a bark followed by a roar from a pit bull pouncing on our dogs. Everyone was screaming.

I yanked up my dogs, but it was complete chaos. My dogs swung in the air with the pit bull lunging after. The pit bull bit into Ruby, who screamed in agony. The next moment, it had my smaller dog in its mouth. Rocky's so small, God, he won't last. Rocky somehow slipped out of his harness and took off for the busy intersection.

God, what do I do? It happened in a moment before my mind had time to process it. I ran after Rocky to see where he was running. I couldn't keep up and lost sight of him. I ran back to Mike and the boys. Mike's hand was bit trying to free the dogs. Thank GOD the boys were untouched. I ran to get the car, and picked up Mike, the boys, and a torn-up Ruby. Ruby's leg was sliced open with her skin hanging off. Mike called the cops while my older son, Tytus, and I looked for Rocky. We searched for hours without success.

I pulled into the driveway, defeated. I saw the leash with Rocky's harness still attached. It was bloody. My heart sank. I started crying, and Tytus collapsed on me. Why did this nightmare happen?

The next days were a blur of searching, postings online, and talking to people who helped us search. I was beyond frustrated. I spent so much time searching. I'd lost my voice calling for him. I felt guilty every second I wasn't searching. Is he alive? He slept with us, and I couldn't sleep knowing he may be out there.

Each day, more hope was lost. A storm hit, and temperatures dropped below freezing. There's no way he'd still be alive. Fears plagued me. "Did someone find him and keep him? Should we hire a tracker? Where would he go? Would that picture of him running away be the last time I see him? Why would someone let their pit bull out?"

The attack replayed in my mind. The house the pit bull came from was next door to my childhood church. The very same church where I invited God into my life. It felt personal and dark, like an attack from the enemy. I'd seen him do this before. Our enemy prowls in the dark to seek who he can steal, kill and destroy. He sends us, like Rocky, reeling into hiding.

I knew God had a purpose in the pain, so I cried out to Him. I begged God to let Rocky come home. It was Easter week. The only hunting my children were doing was searching for their beloved one-year-old puppy.

I opened my Bible to where I was reading with the kids. In 1 Samuel 9, Samuel anointed Saul as king. Saul was looking for his lost donkeys, and the words in verse 20 leaped off the page, "And by the way, your lost donkeys, the ones you've been hunting for the last three days, have been found, so don't worry about them." I started counting the days. It's been three days Rocky's been missing. *Is this what You wanted me to read?* I invited the kids to pray with me.

The next morning was Good Friday, and I told Mike we needed to pray. I ended my prayer with, "It would certainly be a good Friday if we found Rocky." Right after we prayed, the phone rang. It was an officer reporting that someone spotted a Yorkie less than a mile from our home.

What are the odds after four days? We flew to the location and pulled up to a lady that pointed across the street to a big storm drainage. My eyes fiercely searched until I locked eyes on my Rocky! I couldn't believe it! He was alive! *Thank You, God! You do love me, and I feel it at this moment. You answered my prayers, and You did this just for me. My heart feels whole as You've restored something that was lost. You allowed me to feel love deeper because of the pain.*

I told the story at CR, as so many had looked for Rocky. We were blown away by the support of our community who searched for our puppy. This unique situation allowed me to experience love, kindness, and healing from the community. Each week at CR, we select a verse from the bag, and I read my randomly chosen verse. Galatians 5:1, "Christ has set us free to life a free life. So take your stand! Never again let anyone put a harness of slavery on you." The picture of Rocky's bloody harness came to mind. I felt a link in the chain fall to the ground. Free indeed.

July 27, 2022

I haven't heard from the board in months, so I reached out. They responded that I'd hear something by September. My heart sank. I'd been praying I'd have a hearing set by September, not brushed off for another six months. That puts me a year past my eligibility. Had I known it was backed up this long, I'd have submitted it earlier. I started this process seven years ago.

A pardon doesn't take the crime away, but it's no longer held against me. I'll always have a past full of consequences. It's the label that tethers me to my past and prevents me from fully moving forward. The law, rumors, papers, rejections, restrictions, isolations, chains, bars, judgments, rules, and travel blocks weigh me down. I'm thrown into a sex offender box to be judged. Someone put a lid on it and declared, "She's done for." God called me to break out of that box. My pardon is the final step.

I'm reading a book about thanking God for everything. I wondered, "Have I ever truly thanked God for prison?" I knew God would work it all out for good to glorify Himself and help others. I didn't know if I could muster up all the strength in the world to thank Him for being locked up.

"God (gulp), thank You for putting prison in Your plan for my life. I don't understand it, but I trust You. I know You're good and for me. There's much I didn't receive, and You needed to rebuild my foundation on You alone. You did much of that in prison. You gave me time and space by eliminating many distractions. I discovered You for who You are. It's no longer who the church says You are. Thank You for the rejections. All the door slamming made Your way for me crystal clear. You led me to my former church, where I received much healing. I flourished in coordinating for Angel Tree. There was much life there, but also death. In that death, You led me to our church now, where I received healing and freedom from alcohol. Rejection from both public and private school systems brought homeschooling into our lives. We have reaped many rewards with homeschooling, as it was Your plan."

August 29, 2022

For the past eight years, my pardon process has taken me through three governors, four assistants, and three sheriffs. That's just the waiting season. One year ago, they said it could take up to a year for them to get to me. It's been four months past that.

September is almost here, so I bit the bullet and asked the status of my pardon. Their words sliced and diced my hopeful heart. I'd hear something in another nine months. There wasn't any explanation, just more rejection and push back.

I watched my pardon tunnel sweep further out of reach. The massive mountain I have yet to climb moved further into the distance once again. Hurt and anger replaced my hope. It triggered my charge, lies, labels, and restrictions. I felt alone with my thoughts without anyone who can understand.

I hit the ground running and upped my PR from sixteen miles to eighteen. It helped to pound it out in God's presence. The more Mike tried to draw near to my hurt, the more I self-protected. I didn't realize the shell on my back. I didn't want to crack open for the oozing of hurt and anger. I was a ticking turtle time bomb.

Mike suggested I should enter a marathon, but I didn't want approval from anyone or their awards. Who would've imagined the girl who threw shot and discus in high school would run her first marathon right after she turned forty? Though broken, my heart still beat true and pumped life to accomplish 26.2 miles.

I hit CR that evening and shared. My walls came down as I processed my emotions. That night, I revealed to Mike my struggle. It's what he needed to see and what I needed to lay down. I hate being open and vulnerable. Communicating my feelings hasn't been easy. It still feels like the burning off of my flesh. The difference after eighteen years of marriage is simply that I do it. Sometimes it takes a while, or apparently, for me, running a marathon.

September 17, 2022

I heard God whisper, "Do not harden your heart. Plow up the hard soil of your heart. When you feel your heart dwell on things of the past, come to Me. Don't allow your heart to harden in hurt or anger. I'll take your hard heart and give you a tender and responsive heart." It's difficult to turn into pain. Pain is where life is found, not numbed. I'll often find myself motioning the plowing of my heart. I'll air tear with my fingers over my heart as I pray. Keep me tender and near You, God.

Jeremiah 2:13 says, "My people have done two evil things: They have abandoned me, the fountain of living water. And they have dug for themselves cracked cisterns that can hold no water at all!" I recognized when rejections come, I stop going to the Lord. My enemy is crafty and continues using the same bags of tricks because they work.

It was an epiphany for me. In my rejection, I gave the enemy victory because I stopped going to God. Why? Is it because I'm mad at God, or because I feel He's rejected me, or both? Whenever I stop going to the Lord, I find another place to pour myself into. That place will always be cracked. I continue pouring my unsatisfied self out into something that was never meant to hold me. I seep out all over because nothing but God can hold me.

In my life, I've gone to different places. In marriage, I went to someone else. After parole, I went to overexercising. In my recent rejection pileup, I drank from the cistern of numbing vodka. I never thought I was abandoning God because I always continued in ministry, church, prayer, and Bible reading. It's a slow fade, and eventually, I drift to escaping more and going to God less.

I wondered why God hardened Pharoah's heart so many times. Why so long before the children of Israel could leave Egypt? Hadn't their slavery and suffering been long enough? God selected Moses to deliver the people, so why did Pharaoh keep rejecting Moses? God wants Israel's freedom, so why does He purposely harden Pharoah's heart and prolong it? It seems like God's working against His own plan.

I found the answer in Exodus 7:3: "So I can multiply my miraculous signs and wonders in the land of Egypt." There were more miracles, signs, and wonders God wanted to perform. There was more glory He'd get.

Why won't the board let me go? Why can't I exit my Egypt, and be released from my harness of slavery to the law? I feel just like Moses. I'm at the bottom of the social ranking going up against the ruler of the land.

CHAPTER 22

Healing

January 9, 2023

I had to register today. Another reminder at the beginning of a brand new year that the war still rages against my past. I've walked through much healing in the wait, but I wanted more.

On New Year's Day, I went for a run despite the cold. I asked God for a word for the year and heard Him say, "Sun." Malachi 4:2–3 came to mind, "But for you, sunrise! The sun of righteousness will dawn on those who honor my name, healing radiating from its wings. You will be bursting with energy, like colts frisky and frolicking. And you'll tromp on the wicked. They'll be nothing but ashes under your feet that day. God of Angel Armies says so."

I desired healing to radiate from my body and my past to be nothing but ashes under my feet. The Chris Tomlin song, "Whom

Shall I Fear [God of Angel Armies],"[17] was my theme song through Angel Tree.

January 15, 2023

I struggled with intimacy with God, and I wanted more. Sunday, while in worship, I saw a rope that led through a dark tunnel. I kept putting one hand in front of the other. The tunnel led up, like I'd been underground. When I popped out, I discovered sand and the ocean beyond.

I felt God ask me to go forward for prayer, so I shared my struggle with intimacy with the Lord. As Joyce prayed, I saw myself back in that tunnel, holding onto the rope. I looked down and saw chains attached to my body. I followed the rope that led me out of that darkness. I came out from under the sand by the seashore. I continued following the rope as I prayed through declarations of freedom over my past and the release of its punishment. I'm a daughter of King and no longer under the law.

The rope led under a large waterfall. Joyce said, "Walk under the waterfall and be washed from the past." She had no idea the picture God played in my mind. I walked underneath the mighty flood that drenched me from head to toe. I prayed for restoration in all the places I couldn't see. After the water cleared, I could see the sun. I actually felt it on my skin. "Sun" was my word, and it danced with a warm welcome. As they prayed, I felt lighter. I lifted upright, little by little, out of my coiled position. I now stood with Jesus. He was wrapped in light, holding a torch-like scepter, lighting the way. I prayed, "Jesus, stay close and fill me. I don't want to go back, fill in all my holes."

---

[17] "Whom Shall I Fear [God of Angel Armies]," *Burning Lights,* (Sparrow Records; Chris Tomlin), 2012.

Later that afternoon, I opened my Bible where I had left off in Psalm 84:1–5. The section was titled "Pilgrim's Journey" in my Message version. "And how blessed all those in whom you live, whose lives become roads you travel. They wind through lonesome valleys, come upon brooks, discover cool springs and pools brimming with rain! God traveled these roads curve up the mountain and the last turn— Zion! God in full view! God of the Angel Armies, listen: O God of Jacob open your ears—I'm praying! Look at our shields, glistening in the SUN, our faces shining with your gracious anointing. One day spent in your house, This beautiful place of worship beats thousands spent on Greek island beaches. I'd rather scrub floors in the house of my God than be honored as a guest in the palace of sin. The LORD God is our SUN and our shield. He gives us grace and glory. The LORD will withhold no good thing from those who do what is right."

God never left me when I walked through the lonesome valley of prison. I came out of the ground and discovered the beauty of resting in His presence. I saw the sun shining over the mountain of the pardon before me. I prayed God would anoint me as we approached the board together.

He alone is my life source. I'm ready for the next step into my pardon and on to Florida. As amazing as that'll be, it won't bring lasting peace or happiness. God alone is my SUN. I desire to receive fullness from the Son into the Sunshine State. Like Moses said, "If You're not with me, I'm not going."

I prayed, "I don't just want deliverance; I want the Deliverer. I don't just want the remedy; I want the Redeemer. I don't just want healing; I want the Healer. I don't just want freedom; I want the Freedom Fighter. I don't just want victory; I want the Victor. I don't just want restoration; I want the Restorer. I don't just want the way; I want the Way Maker. I don't want to just feel the Sun; I want to know the Son.

In my desperation, I seek so much from You, but ultimately, what I need is more of You. My season, situation, and circumstances will change. My hope and prayer are that I won't be fighting my pardon battle and past restrictions forever, though it feels like it. There'll be more challenges up ahead. I need You. I need the closeness. I need a forever suntan. I want all of You, and more.

January 17, 2023

I felt some kind of a release happen Sunday. I want to stay free. I heard God say, "You agreed with a lie." When I went forward for prayer, I had pictured chains on my wrists and ankles. The chains, labels, restrictions, registrations, rejections, isolation, sentencing, Segregation, public humiliation, strip-searching, treatment centers, mental institution, prison, Work Release, ankle monitor, parole, and tests all burned and branded me. Every program, school, ministry, church, society, and what people said about me affirmed it.

I thought I was what everyone thought of me. My shame kept that monster strapped to my back. I lived my life under that label rather than my true identity in Christ. I tried to get this heavy load off time and time again. I constantly fought the lie with each slap of rejection, but I grew defeated. I even tried outrunning the rejection, but I can't run that far. No one can.

I had lived a lie that was embedded into my skin by shame. Though I loathed it, I allowed the lie to stay because I thought I had to let it remain. James 5:16, "Confess your faults one to another and pray for each other that you may be healed. The earnest prayer of a righteous person has great power and produces wonderful results." Big lies need big prayers. I desired freedom on this side of the pardon. John 8:36, "So if the Son sets you free, you will be free indeed."

Head knowledge can be a trap. You think because you know something, you actually believe it. Even Satan knows there's a God, but he doesn't worship Him. Do I live out what I think? If I really believed with every fiber of my being, then I'd live like it. My mind is a battlefield. Until what I know settles the eighteen inches from my mind to my heart, it'll never take root in my life.

Rejection cuts me most and leaves wounds like no other. Rejection cuts you off like a castaway. I've felt shunned, despised, thrown away, and worthless. If we struggle to find acceptance from the church or people we can see, I believe we will struggle to find acceptance from a God we can't see. In my severest rejection, I rejected God.

I know I've resented God for not protecting me from situations. I've seen Him like the judge who sentenced me. I've doubted His protection and relied on myself too many times to count. I've rejected God's love, thinking I didn't deserve it and that He condemned me. I've turned a cold shoulder to God and responded to fears instead. I may have never said these words out loud, but I believed them.

God is merciful and gentle to process with me a little at a time. When the wounds and pain run deep, it's too much to deal with at once. I've journeyed through deep trenches of rejection and received much healing, but there's more to come. How do I stop the negative feelings of rejection? I certainly can't control others or the law, but I can control my mind by renewing it in the Word.

Romans 8:1, "There is now no condemnation for those that are in Christ Jesus." I'm NOT who the law says I am. God alone is the true judge and has forgiven me. I must remember Jesus was rejected and knows how I feel. I often discount it because He was innocent, and I'm not. None of us are innocent, though. There's no hierarchy of sin. It all nailed Jesus to the cross and cost Him His life. It's because of His great love He declares me righteous like Him.

When I forget or lose sight of this truth, I slip back into what the law says. For me, that's death. The truth is that I'm free. If I don't stand on the freedom Jesus paid for with His blood, then I'll put my old chains back on. Why would I do that? It's because I listen to another voice instead of God's. Satan is the father of lies. When our enemy breathes lies down our neck, we must remember who we are.

Simba from The Lion King had forgotten who he was. Rafiki finds Simba in hiding and asks the famous question, "Who are you?" Simba says he thought he knew, but doesn't know anymore.

Then Simba hears words from his father, "You have forgotten who you are, and so forgotten me. You are more than who you've become. You must take your place. Remember who you are. You are my son."

Preach, Mufasa. When we leave God out of our lives, we forget who we are.

Romans 8:31–34, "If God is for us, who can be against us? Since He did not spare even his own son but gave him up for us all, won't he also give us everything else? Who dares accuse us whom God has chosen for HIs own? No one—for God Himself has given us right standing with Himself. Who then will condemn us? No one—for Christ Jesus died for us and was raised to life for us, and he is sitting in the place of honor at God's right hand, pleading for us."

I must live in truth and live my life for an audience of One.

January 21, 2023

Anger set in. All at once, everything irritated me. I cleaned, cooked, exercised, and even thrift-shopped. Thumbing through the clothes, I felt a deep sadness. I heard God whisper, "You are mad."

I replied, "I don't want to be mad. I want to be healed."

"This is part of it," He said.

I wanted more healing, so I had to work through more pain. Anger is part of it.

Later, I asked God what I was angry about. I wanted the root of my anger and felt He said, "protection." I'm upset when I feel unprotected. The truth is that God could have protected me from this pain. Everything I've walked through has felt like it's been the worst-case scenario, and His beloved daughter sits rejected for two decades. I felt my heart reject some of what my mind was trying to tell it. I was frustrated.

I listened to the song "The Goodness of God."[18] What stands out is, "I've known You as a Father; I've known You as a Friend." As a child, I desperately wanted someone with me. I invited Jesus into my heart and felt Him cover me when I was bullied at school or scared at home. I had ongoing conversations in my mind with Him. He was truly my invisible friend.

I don't know if I've experienced Him as a Father as I should have. I think this relates to my struggle with feeling protected. I've felt responsibility for my family like a parent rather than a child. I've also been wounded by several pastors on epic levels.

January 23, 2023

I worked through writing anger letters. It's an exercise I've done before to move past the anger. I made connections and identified some roots from the lies I've heard. I need to chop down the roots to keep the anger plants from growing.

The Bible says that unsettled anger doesn't stop there. Ephesians 4:31, "Get rid of all bitterness, rage and anger, brawling and slander, along with every form of malice." The Amp version says, "Resentment, fault finding, strife, verbal abuse, hostility, friction, loud talking, contention, not letting things go, bad temper, and ill will toward another." The longer I sit in anger, the more control it has over me. Ephesians 4:26, "Be angry, yet do not sin. Do not let the

---

[18] "Goodness of God" *Victory,* (Bethel Music; Jenn Johnson), 2019.

sun set upon your anger." How angry I get over the little stuff is a good indication of how angry I am.

Anger is like the fire alarm going off. It tells me there's a fire, but I have to find it and put it out. Anger isn't wrong, as it's a God-given emotion. It's what I do with the anger that may lead to sin. The goal is to work through the anger and get to the root. I have to find the fire. I'm angry the enemy keeps attacking with shame and lies. I'm angry I still have to register as a sex offender after doing everything anyone has asked of me. I served my time in prison, a mental institution, parole, and over a decade of registering. It's never enough, and I feel unprotected.

I've learned shame and guilt are two different things. Guilt is a result of feeling convicted about something we did that we shouldn't, and we haven't confessed it yet. As 1 John 1:9 says, once we confess sin to God, we are forgiven and set free from it.

Shame is an identity, label, or mask I wear because of my past. When I ask Jesus to forgive me, He does. My enemy comes and drapes what I did over my shoulders like a heavy cloak weighing me down. Then he speaks lies over me. My shame is my label as a registered sex offender. I can't remove the label society has branded me with.

After going forward for prayer last week, I felt a release of shame. I pictured chains coming off my body. The cloak of heaviness was lifted. The pardon doesn't free me. Only Jesus frees me. Circumstances never guarantee happiness, victory, or fulfillment; only Jesus does. I have all I need right now, despite my circumstances. Freedom is mine for the taking. The struggle comes when I'm reminded of my past. I have to take each thought captive and make it obey the truth (2 Corinthians 10:5).

When I surround myself with light, I not only feel better, I am better. When I bask in His presence, truth, praise, and healthy people, I'm lifted up out of the pit. Truth dispels darkness, and I can see clearly.

When I saturated myself in Scripture in prison, I was better. When I flooded my mind with praise songs when I ran, I was better. When I wrote all my pain and invited God into the pain, instead of drowning myself in vodka, I was better. When I confessed my struggles to healthy believers in the presence of God, I was healed from past wounds I could never remove.

I have this bad habit of wearing my contacts as long as I can. I struggled to read my Bible and finally decided I needed to let this pair go and get a new pair. As I put in my new contacts, God said, "Fresh eyes." When we can't see the way, we need to yield to God. Reading the Bible gives us fresh eyes to see what's right in front of us.

February 19, 2023

There was a revival in Kentucky. Our message was on revival, complete with an altar call. I went forward and sat before the altar like a kindergartener at carpet time. I asked God to revive my heart and draw me closer to Him. Revival means "Awake." I've definitely heard that before. In my mind, I saw a golden rope released down to me from above. I took the rope and climbed up to the extended hand. It was Jesus, and He had more healing as I sat in His presence.

As I prayed God would fill me with more of Himself, I felt the muscles around my lungs expanding. I continued praying, and my body lifted little by little until I was sitting up straight. It wasn't weird, but I felt different. Things that typically weighed me down didn't bother me. I felt confident in who I was in Christ. The past seemed beneath me. I prayed, "Don't let things attach to me; let it all roll off." In my mind, I saw the shame attacks hitting lower on my body and falling off. Shame was unable to attach to my shoulders like a weighted cloak. I'm free and want to stay free.

Pastor read Hebrews 12:1–3: "Therefore, since we are surrounded by such a great cloud of witnesses, let us throw off everything that hinders and the sin that so easily entangles. And let us run with perseverance the race marked out for us, fixing our eyes on Jesus, the pioneer and perfecter of faith. For the joy set before him he endured the cross, scorning its shame, and sat down at the right hand of the throne of God. Consider him who endured such opposition from sinners, so that you will not grow weary and lose heart."

The phrase "Scorning the shame" repeated in my mind. I pictured Jesus fighting for me against the shame that tries to attach itself to me. I saw Him angry, like when He chased the money changers out of His Father's house. My dad would get angry like that and fight for me. That must be what the phrase means.

Later, I looked it up. Scorn means "Disregard, dismiss, or ignore." I'll admit, I was disappointed. It seemed like Jesus didn't care. But after thinking about it, I've discovered my initial feelings couldn't be further from the truth. Jesus didn't give shame power. Jesus didn't get angry because it wasn't worth His time. He doesn't give shame access to His emotions. It had zero control over Him. It doesn't get to move Him and rolls off like nothing.

Shame is nothing compared to the love and joy of dying for us and fulfilling His plan to redeem us. Jesus endured more opposition than I do. His opposition crucified Him. He understands, so I can't give up. I need to focus on Jesus and not on the shame.

February 24, 2023

We watched the final service of the Asbury revival. What stood out most was how we are forever changed by revival. When we experience the presence of the Lord, we are different. We've been awakened and free from sin's power.

Bella couldn't sleep that night, so I prayed over her. As I prayed, I was overcome by the love of God in the gift of my Bella. God birthed her into my life when I needed it most. Our marriage wasn't in a good place at the end of Work Release. I'd allowed lies to settle, and they attacked viciously. Bella was there when I hit my rock bottom at the bottom of the bottle. She loves me no matter what. God led me to pray for leadership, love, compassion, and a longing heart for Jesus over her. We were both wrecked in an awesome way.

The next morning, I awoke to my ten-year-old son coming to snuggle. Tytus longs to be in my presence. God whispered that He longs for that from us. Like Tytus, God wants us to run to Him with everything. He wants us to snuggle in close and talk to Him. He wants to share the keys to life with us in His word. His Word fills in every nook and cranny of our hearts.

Tytus relishes lingering a little while longer with Mom without all her distractions, just him and me. It fills his bucket with love, peace, and wholeness. That's the same with God, but on a much grander scale, as He is God. God is a healer, and He releases healing and transformation in His presence. His presence is where it's at.

I felt led to share with Tytus about my past. I tailored it for his young mind to process. I watched the gaps fill in his mind as he asked, "Is that why we haven't moved to Florida yet?" I was again overwhelmed by God's love with the gift of my firstborn redheaded son. He loves me fiercely and unconditionally. He cried with me and hugged me the entire time.

After I shared, he said there were some things he wanted to ask God's forgiveness for, so we prayed. That's the same response almost every time I share my story, from the smallest to the tallest of people. People who hear my story share their story with me. There's power and healing like James 5:16 declares, "Confess your sins to each other and pray for each other so that you may be healed. The earnest prayer of a righteous person is powerful and effective."

Good Friday, 2023

Today, we remember that Jesus shouldered the weight of the entire world's sin on His shoulders and died for us. Our family also celebrates the one-year return of our Rocky. I personally celebrate the lavish love of God in all things, big and small.

The pardon's board failed to meet this quarter. They only meet four times a year, so half the year will be over before they meet again. I don't understand why the board pushed me back almost three years beyond when they said to return. I commit to trusting God and listening to Him alone.

Joel 3:21, "I will pardon my people's crimes which I have not yet pardoned; and I, the LORD, will make my home in Jerusalem with my people." I'm thankful for God's presence through this long and weary battle. He gives strength to rise above my circumstances as He promised in Isaiah 40:31, "Those who trust in the LORD will find new strength. They will soar high on wings like eagles. They will run and not grow weary. They will walk and not faint." It reminds me of the butterfly I saw in Segregation.

Just thinking about entering the Capitol and approaching the board again sends my heart into a crippling fear. I've prayed for God to take the fears away, and He has transformed those chambers into a room of praise by giving me a new picture as I pray for my pardon.

I stand next to Jesus like in Psalm 46:5, "God is in the midst of her; she shall not be moved: God shall help her, and that right early." We are ready to walk down the aisle toward the board. Jesus holds His scepter high with radiating light piercing through the darkness. I'm in the same white gown I've seen, but large, beautiful wings unfold like a butterfly. The wings sweep light around us like a shield of protection. My burden became my wings. The same rejection Satan meant to destroy me with, Jesus uses to lift me beyond and experience new heights.

With each step I take, the wings unfurl until they've filled the cold room with light and splendor. Though I stand before the board, I have the approval of God. Like Joseph's colorful coat, my wings display that I'm radically loved. My focus isn't on the board, but behind their heads. Above them is God. I stand before them, because of Him. Isaiah 40:1–2, "Comfort, oh comfort my people," says your God. "Speak softly and tenderly to Jerusalem, but also make it very clear that she has served her sentence, that her sin is taken care of— forgiven and pardoned! She's been punished enough and more than enough, and now it's over and done with."

Isaiah 53: 5, "He was pierced for our transgressions, he was crushed for our iniquities; the punishment that brought us peace was on him, and by his wounds, we are healed."

I thank God for this Good Friday and that I'm free on this side of the pardon. It may feel like Friday, but my Sunday is coming.

NEXT STEPS

I hope my story of God's redemptive power inspires you to rise out of the prison of past shame, pain, and rejection. Assume your true identity as a chosen child of God and get to know your Father. Never allow people to skew your view of Him, for He is who He says He is. No church is perfect and believers will let us down. Stay connected to a body of believers and community. Pursue His Word and His presence and He will change you from the inside out. Never stop forging ahead, even through the trenches. Two steps forward and one step back is still moving in the right direction. God uses suffering and hardships to change, strengthen, and draw us to Himself and others. He can change the trajectory of our lives and the lives of our children, so fan the flames of His desire and call on your heart and set this world on fire for Him.

ChainsToChosen.com

Thank You for Reading
RELEASED!

I really appreciate all of your feedback and
I love hearing what you have to say.

I need your input to make the next version of this
book and my future books better.

Please take two minutes now to
leave a helpful review on

Amazon letting me know what
you thought of the book:

ChainsToChosen.com

Thanks so much!

—Brandy Reynolds

ACKNOWLEDGMENTS

I thank God for His persistent, yet gentle nudging to write my story. Thank you for Your presence. You never left me alone one second of my life and encompassed me through the valleys of the shadows of death. Thank you for redeeming my past to display your amazing love and grace. Thank you for the freedom and healing birthed from writing. May it bring freedom and healing to others. All the glory is Yours!

I thank my husband Michael, who remained my rock through our 19 years of marriage. Thank you for never giving up on me in my darkest places. You breathe stability into my world and I'm forever grateful for our marriage and three amazing children.

I thank my daughter Isabella. You are a gift Mommy greatly needed and the "one up" God used to move me. Your sweet innocence radiated my change. God entrusted you into my life and knew I'd be better for it. You amaze me and will be a better version of me. Thank you for believing in me and loving me without measure.

I thank my firstborn son, Tytus. Thank you for being my biggest fan and defending me, no matter how wrong I am. Your unwavering faith in me makes me think that there's nothing I can't do.

I thank my Christmas baby Jacob. You remind me to seek adventure and live life to the fullest. God can move mountains and breathed you into my heart before you were even born. You are a miracle from the miracle-working God.

I thank my ride or die Sierra Michael. God orchestrated us sitting next to each other at MOPS. Just like Mike, God assigned you the seat right next to me. You've never left my side since, including my alcohol addiction. Thank you for not leaving when others did. I'm certain God has a crown for you and Mike for walking through that. Maybe the archangel Michael will give it to you both.

I thank my mother-in-law and lifeline Cheryl, who wrote me the most. I appreciate you tremendously for always being there even though you were states away. Thank you for rallying your women troops from Bible study who wrote me and countless others in prison. Your words and prayers were straight from the heart of God.

I thank my parents, sisters, sisters-in-law, and all those who wrote and visited me in prison. Your visits, words, encouragement and support strengthened me day in and day out to walk through the trenches. Thank you for shouldering my burden and loving me well.

I thank Al and Nadine Peters for coming to York each Monday night for Bible study. Your constant encouragement and love were God's presence in a very dark place. Thank you for your faithfulness to love those in prison and make them a priority.

I thank Steve and Diane Collins as well as the other ministries that preach truth and hope on Sunday mornings in prison. Your life, testimony and words, "You will still do great things for Christ," marked me. I too desire to bring hope to those desperate for Jesus. Thank you for your gifts, time and encouragement.

Thank you to my prison friends who shared their lives, pain, and hearts with me. Thank you JoAnna Langston for inviting me into your family. Mom Peggy, thank you for the rides to work each day with a banana and OJ for me and my belly baby Bella. You love like Jesus and made me feel human while I was in your car.

I thank my prison mentor Tara Rye. I only met you a few short months before my sentencing. After hearing you pray, I knew you were the real deal. I joined your study, but never got a chance to finish. Thank you for sending me studies in prison, being at my parole hearing, writing, and praying.

I thank my post prison mentor, Suzette Davis, who spoke life into me in such a profound way. Your loving gift of dispelling lies and revealing truth reaps inevitable change. Thank you for leading Break Free and inviting me along every path you walked in your brief time in Nebraska. I miss following your lead.

I thank my sidekick, Josie Smith. You were my angel in Angel Tree with your mad event-coordinating skills. You put into place visions that only existed in my mind. Thank you for editing my pardon application and being my sounding board in leading CrossRoads ministry groups. We were stronger together and pulled off some pretty amazing God-sized stuff.

I thank Pastor Mike Wenig, who resembles more of Jesus than anyone I know. You weep with those who weep. When you cried with my friend who delivered stillborn twins, it impacted me immensely. Thank you for sticking up for me. Thank you for treating me like a child of God and not a registered sex offender.

I thank all my MOPS friends. I had no idea how much I would need and love you. You are my people, and I praise God I had such amazing women in my corner. You were my church. I felt at home with each of you and hold you as a precious gift forever. Thank you, Vickie Goebel, who encouraged me to step into leading. I was afraid, and you pioneered my way through when I faltered. Thank you, Marlene Jacobus and Hilary Mason, for fighting for me when I have no fight left.

I thank Becky Marshall, my Celebrate Recovery leader, and all those in CR. Thank you for being a safe place without judgment. CR was my saving grace, especially during my first year of sobriety. Thank you for welcoming everyone without strings attached.

I thank Robert and Joyce Wilson, who plead to God on my behalf and prayed over me like I've never experienced. I needed you. God redeemed much with you pastoring me. Thank you for your faithfulness to Him and for starting a church in Fremont. I know it wasn't just for me, but it sure felt like God did it just for me.

I thank all my friends in all the studies I've led over the years. I may have "led" the group, but God led many of you to love, listen, pray, and shepherd me. You sustained me. God heard your prayers and moved for you. I know why God calls you prayer warriors. With my whole heart, thank you.

I thank Jeannie Culbertson, the Noteworthy Mom, for her guidance with my story and turning my mess into a message.

ABOUT THE AUTHOR

Brandy Reynolds was born and raised in Nebraska and has over 20 years of experience serving in ministry. She is a devoted wife and homeschooling mother of three children, and is passionate about her faith in Jesus. Brandy loves spending time at the beach and adores her three adorable Yorkie dogs. Through her writing, she encourages and inspires others by sharing her own personal journey and offering hope. Her love for family and unwavering faith are at the heart of her work.

Find Brandy at ChainsToChosen.com to read her latest writings, stay updated, and find bonus materials.